CLAYHANGER
A Wartime Childhood

by
NANCY DE CHAZAL

DEDICATION

In memory of Harry O'Neill Drew 1931 - 1989

My brother

ISBN 0 9526375 0 2

Published by Nancy de Chazal
Sydling St. Nicholas
Dorchester
DT2 9NX

Printed by Creeds the Printers, Broadoak, Bridport DT6 5NL

CONTENTS

1.	Arrival	p. 1
2.	The Rectory	p. 4
3.	The Garden and Glebe	p. 15
4.	Callers	p. 23
5.	School	p. 28
6.	Beach Court School	p. 38
7.	The Village and People	p. 53
8.	The Parish	p. 60
9.	Animals	p. 65
10.	Outings and Holidays	p. 76
11.	The War	p. 86
12.	Postscript	p. 96

Chapter 1.   ARRIVAL

Glorious Devon

> Dorset, Somerset, Cornwall, Wales,
> May envy the likes of we,
> For the flow'r of the West, the first, the best,
> The pick o' the bunch us be;
> Squab pie, junket, and cyder brew,
> Richest of cream from the cow,
> What'd Old England without 'em do?
> And where 'ud 'un be to now?
> As crumpy as a lump of lead
> Be a loaf without good leaven,
> And the yeast Mother England do use for her bread
> Be Devon,
> Be Devon, glorious Devon.
>   Harold Boulton.

On 6th. November 1939 we left St. Helens in the pouring rain, a grimy drab and large industrial town, smelling of soot and Beecham's pills. We had been there less than two years while our father had been curate of a large parish in the suburb of Eccleston. November 5th. had been disappointing to children as no bonfires or fireworks were allowed that year because of the war. In any case it had poured with rain. However, we ate delicious parkin made every bonfire night. As far as I remember we never ate it any other time of year. It was made in a deep baking tin from oats and treacle, and some years was soft and spongy and other years hard and tacky and broke ones teeth. Associated for ever with the smell of smoke and the noise of minor explosions.

Early in the morning Pickford's van arrived to carry away the furniture from the small curate's house where we lived. We ourselves left later in the day by train, our most valuable possession, Timmy, yowling in his basket in the guard's van. A long, rambling wartime journey, clanking down through the midlands and shunting round Crewe, smoke and rain and long delays. The journey lasted all day, and marked a major turning point in our lives, leaving behind for ever the grime, poverty and illness associated in my mind with St. Helens. Although we were only small children, those two years in the north had made a deep impression. Our mother had come from Lancashire and the Isle of Man and we had relations in Bolton and Liverpool, but it always seemed strange to us, children from the south. Our father had been curate in a large parish in a poor suburb. There was great and noticeable poverty. It was the time of unemployment and the dole, of fever hospitals and the death of children. The woman next door was the sole breadwinner of her family, and her daughter, my age, was dying of TB. In the streets of the parish children played without shoes. Harry and I had been very ill there with scarlet fever followed by diptheria early in 1939, and that, plus the outbreak of war, persuaded our parents to move.

Our father's ancestors had come from Cornwall, and when he was offered a living in the wilds of Devon, he rushed south on a flying visit, and seeing a quiet and peaceful hamlet slumbering in the sun, accepted thankfully.

We spent the night in Taunton, and the following day trundled along the Barnstable line to Venn Cross, where we were met by the Churchwarden, Mr. Elworthy, a farmer. With him we went up along and down along the lanes to the scattered hamlet of Clayhanger in the Blackdown hills. The rain came down in sheets and streams ran along the sides of the road. It was to rain pretty steadily for the next seven weeks, in spite of which we fell lastingly in love with Devon.

There were a number of practical difficulties to settling down in the heart of the country in wartime Britain. We had left a small curate's house lit by electricity, served by piped water, linked to the main drains. We arrived two days later at a Regency rectory, linked by passages to the original Elizabethan house at the back. We furnished as much of the front of the house as possible, and by late afternoon waved away the removal men cheerfully.

Father had lived all his life in houses supplied with water and drains. In his earliest childhood he remembers gas lights, but they were soon changed to electric light. Clayhanger Rectory was much the same as when it was originally built, apart from the Regency addition,, and all former graciousness of living had been supplied by a large domestic staff, now vanished from the scene. It was not until the men had left and the day began to close in, that our parents began to realize the situation. There was no water. At least indoors. The rain continued unabated outside. We explored the house again, all three floors, except for a mysterious locked room, dark when viewed through the keyhole. No bathroom. There were two sinks, one of shallow brownstone in the kitchen, one deep white porcelain in the Butler's Pantry (as marked on the plan). Both had single taps which coughed out a trickle of brownish liquid, obviously old rain water. Harry and I were not particularly interested in the lack of water for washing, but didn't much care for the idea of going to bed in an isolated mansion in the dark. For there was no light either. The rooms were beautiful, their clear lines unsullied by wires or switches or hanging bulbs. Our mother, used to cooking on gas, was standing in the kitchen rather gloomily surveying an ancient and dilapidated cooking range.

In the last of the light we went in our thin shoes and macks with father to look for help. The rectory lay in three acres of ground half a mile from the village. Not a flat walk, but up and down through shadowed banks. We called at the nearest farm and borrowed two buckets and some candles. The farmer thought us pretty improvident we could tell. He sent someone with us to show us our well. A couple of hundred yards from the house down a steepish road, or closer down a vertical bank was a deep and moss-lined well open to the skies, where we filled our buckets and staggered home with the icy water. As far as I remember, we went twice a day with the two buckets. Our consumption of water sharply dropped as we realized its value fully for the first time. There were no more daily baths. Apart from the water situation, there was no bath. We found some saucers and stuck the candles in, and so to bed.

After St. Helens the most noticeable thing about Clayhanger was the complete quiet. The village was served by a third class road, leading from and to other equally small villages. There was no traffic. All we heard the first night was the steady drum of the rain on the courtyard and windows, and in the early morning the mooing of the cows as they went along the road below us.

Before breakfast we were back again at the farm for milk. But none was to be had. No milk! Father was incredulous. What about the cows? It was wartime. All milk was under contract, and the farmer had no licence to sell direct. What did the people in the village drink? Tinned milk. Or occasionally skimmed milk. Apart from the labourer who was entitled to milk, none could afford the fresh supply, produced all around them in the rich green pastures of Devon. So poverty was not less here than in the towns, although less noticeable. For today, he would let us have some of his, and would apply for a permit to sell it. We went home carrying a little churn, a great improvement on the milkman.

It seems incredible looking back now after a further fifty years close connection with the Church of England, the speed at which things happened then. We had arrived on 7th. November, and in the afternoon of Wednesday 8th. November our father was instituted as Rector of the living of Clayhanger, and Perpetual Curate of Petton, by the Bishop of Exeter. We had arrived and taken our place in a new and unknown society.

Chapter 2.   THE RECTORY

Intimations of Immortality

There was a time when meadow, grove and stream,
The earth, and every common sight,
To me did seem
Apparalled in celestial light,
The glory and the freshness of a dream.
It is not now as it hath been of yore;
Turn wheresoe'er I may,
By night or day,
The things which I have seen I now can see no more.
                                William Wordsworth.

The first few days after father's institution we made lists and picniced. Not outside, of course, because of the rain, but in the house. The house was cold. It had stood empty before our arrival for some months, and the winter, although not cold, was wet. It was the first winter of the war, and everyone was conscious of conforming to the blackout regulations. Our furniture and curtaining were inadequate for the largeness of the house, and our mother insufficiently prepared by father for the difference in size and convenience from our previous home. Until a sweep arrived the antiquated ruin in the kitchen was unusable. So at the head of her list she wrote 'oil stove'. Strangely, to us, this was followed by the words 'bath' and 'wash basins'. Having been provided with such a heavenly place to live in, it seemed rather unnecessary to import such items into a house where people had lived quite happily without them for some 400 years. Harry's list and mine had one item only, 'wellingtons', indispensible to the detailed exploration of the Devon countryside on which we had already embarked.

Early on the Saturday morning of our first week, we made a major expedition to Tiverton. This, our nearest sizable shopping place, was only nine miles away, and now would be considered a short run in a car of twenty minutes or so, even along the third class 'serviceable' roads which linked us to it. But in 1939 and throughout the war, it was very difficult to reach. So difficult and time-consuming in fact, that we only went a few times a year. We found it much easier and more convenient to go to Taunton, twenty miles away in Somerset. First of all we went by hired car the two miles to Venn Cross, where we took the Barnstable train to the next but one station, Morebath Junction Halt, where we changed into the Exeter train and trundled slowly down the upper reaches of the Exe valley through lovely wooded hills sloping down to the water meadows.

House from the South.

Courtyard from garden.

House from North – vegetable garden and Elizabethan wing.

The train crossed and recrossed the valley, stopping at every station to pick up more passengers and chat with local porters and station masters. Between Morebath and Tiverton we stopped at six stations, including a longish wait at the larger village of Bampton to take on some sheep. We had actually had an extra stop at a level crossing to let a large flock of sheep finish crossing the line. I am surprised looking back on those wartime journeys that we have never been referred to as a nation of station masters. Along twenty miles or so of line there were roughly ten station masters, all important, all in hats, all arriving after the train had been greeted by the porter. At Venn Cross there was a station master, porter and signal man, and doubtless the same along the line at other stations. No wonder the gardens were magnificent, bedecked with bright flower beds lined with white painted pebbles.

Eventually we steamed importantly into Tiverton and repaired to the nearest ironmonger for our stores. Here we bought new shiny clanging buckets, a large oil stove with cooker, several plain oil lamps and two elegant lamps for the lounge with incandescent mantles. A major item was a full length galvanized zinc bath, then still on sale in the country towns of England. We added some china ewers and basins for the bedrooms, and candle holders. We already had elegant brass Georgian candlesticks for the hall which had been a wedding present of our grandparents. Now we added plain copper dish candlesticks for our bedrooms and enamelled ones with finger holes for carrying around the downstairs passages. We bought a ten gallon metal container for paraffin and a dozen boxes of candles. Mother saw a primus stove and thought it might come in useful. Especially as it was so easy to use when demonstrated by the ironmonger.

After these major purchases we had lunch in a cafe and went to see the church. It is impossible for father to visit any place for any reason without going to see the church. It was a lovely church, dedicated, as was ours, to St. Peter. Then through the town to Blundells. Before arriving in Devon it had been assumed that Harry would go into the preparatory department of this school, being then just eight years old. This was before the extreme difficulty of a small boy reaching the place daily was realized. Our parents had not yet hardened their hearts to sending him away to school. We all liked what we saw of Blundells through the ever more heavily falling rain. On the way back into the town we bought the wellingtons. Four pairs. And thick socks to go inside. In 1939 small children, neither boys nor girls, wore long trousers. Harry wore grey flannel shorts, shirts and ties and pullovers, and long woollen socks. I wore long-sleeved dresses and long turned back socks. We both had thick green gaberdene coats from a previous school which we were now allowed to use for messing about outside. In the late afternoon father found a lovely old silver table lamp which he bought for the study, and we finished up spending our pocket money in a bookshop. We left Tiverton after dark. I remember sitting in the waiting room with a huge blazing coal fire, reading my book and clutching my new wellingtons. There was a smell of steaming cloth and new rubber. Then the train rushed in, warm and smoky, sparks flying from the engine. We chugged home again, endlessly through the dark countryside, no light showing anywhere, except for the passing of the train.

Sunday morning we attended Matins in Clayhanger Church, dressed in our best clothes. These grew shabbier as the war progressed, and the hats became more dated. All the women and girls of the congregation wore hats, as they had through the centuries since St. Paul. Until the war I had had two new hats a year, apart from school hats. For Easter we had new summer hats, loosely woven of straw and trimmed with flowers. For winter, dome-shaped velvet hats with wide turned-up brims. On sunny afternoons small girls still wore floppy cotton sunbonnets tied under the chin with ribbons. For school we also had two hats, a creamish Panama for summer with the green school ribbon and badge round the brim, and a dark green velour for winter. As the war progressed we began to wear knitted hats, round ones with pom-poms and pixie hoods fastened under the chin with a button.

What a lot of clothes children needed in those days. I started school at the age of five at a small school on the sea front at Walmer, Kent, to which I repaired by bus each day from Deal, price one penny return. In winter we wore cream long-sleeved blouses with green pleated tunics and green cardigans to match, long woollen socks with green stripes and brown lace-up shoes, which we wore with a a thick green overcoat and the velour hat. For gym we changed into green pleated shorts, white ankle socks, white lace-up gym shoes and white short-sleeved blouses. This was taken by an ex-sergeant of the Royal Marines and consisted largely of swinging dumb bells and climbing knotted ropes. Once a week a dancing mistress arrived and we changed into green tussore silk dresses, fawn silk long socks and black dancing pumps. For rainy weather there was a green gaberdene. In summer we wore green and white check cotton dresses with white ankle socks and brown sandals, a green blazer and the Panama. We changed into green bathing costumes for swimming with the ex-sergeant. We were taught to swim in the sea on the end of a long damp knotted rope with which he pulled us into the shore. As it was a very pebbly beach we wore rubber-soled bathing shoes which were always disappearing out to sea. All this clothing was kept by day girls in sizable lockers in the basement marked with our names. As an infant mine had been marked by the picture of a donkey as my initials were NED, the sign of a sense of humour in the infant mistress not appreciated by me. There was also Brownie uniform.

After leaving Deal, father had trained for the ministry at Westcott House, Cambridge, where we joined him for six months before his curacy in St. Helens. In Cambridge we wore the old school uniform, but in St. Helens everything was changed to blue. We still had remnants of the various uniforms in Devon, which we wore in the garden. 1939 was the last year we had completely new outfits twice a year, although Harry's school optimistically listed such items as six grey flannel shirts and worsted shorts and one dozen pairs of grey woollen socks. Mother used to pack his trunk, list in hand, worrying about whether eight pairs would do or not. The matron returning the trunk at the end of term had no such scruples. Everything was flung in willy nilly, no list in sight.

The afternoon of our first Sunday in Clayhanger I walked over to Petton our other church, with father for Evensong at 3 p.m. Evensong was always at three during the winter because of the insoluble problem of blacking out the church. I remember occasions when the hanging oil lamps were lit, but it must have been on dark afternoons. Petton was a tiny hamlet some three miles from Clayhanger. Later we discovered a short cut across the fields of Nutcombe Manor, which cut off over a mile. The road was crossed by the wide stream which flowed through our garden higher up, and a wooden footbridge was provided at the side. Now this has gone, and a new culvert takes the stream under the road. The church at Petton was very small. It had been entirely rebuilt in 1847 as a chapel-of-ease served by Bampton, to which it reverted after father left. There was no village round it, just scattered farms and a few small cottages which provided a tiny congregation. There was a harmonium which wheezed out the hymns reluctantly.

.Towards the end of the following week, the equipment we had bought in Tiverton arrived. Mother was pleased to see the oil stove, although by now the range was in use. A young woman from the village. called Winnie, came each day to work and was to stay almost until we left, until within a few weeks of the birth of her eldest child. She not only helped with the cleaning, but also took home with her our laundry, which was a great help. In the council house where she lived they had the luxury of running water hot and cold from taps. She was good with the range and usually managed to get the temperamental oven to work. For us it was either stone cold or red hot.

Apart from the smell, cooking by oil was just as convenient as gas unless one wanted anything in a hurry. There were three burners and if the oven was wanted, it was lifted onto the stove and balanced over two of them. The wicks were fed by a gallon container of paraffin attached to the side. This made regular gurgling noises. A year or two later a deaf and dumb maid went away and left some hot fat in a frying pan which caught fire as soon as her back was turned. Father found it and flung over it the straw kitchen matting which added to the conflagration. Mother rushed in and bravely took away the full paraffin container and then she and father carried out the blazing stove into the courtyard where it sank into a mouldering ruin in the usual steady drizzle.

The primus stove was set proudly on an enamel topped small table beside the main stove. It was intended for use when quick snacks or cups of tea were needed. Harry and I attended the first demonstration of this marvel. First of all it was pumped rapidly by hand, which caused the paraffin to leak out of the sides of the burner. When a match was applied it was choked by too much paraffin. After several false starts a minor explosion occurred and some of the holes stayed alight, burning with feeble yellow flames and occasional spurts of red. When demonstrated in the shop it had burnt with a fierce purple flame and a steady soothing roar. This was rarely achieved by us, and the primus was demoted to the back scullery and only produced during real emergencies.

That evening we were all anxious to try the new bath. One of the many unfurnished upstairs rooms was designated bathroom, and the bath installed in the middle of the bare wooden boards. A wooden clothes horse was brought in, covered with towels. As it was November, a circular Ripping Gilles oil stove was lit. This was the only spot of luxury in an otherwise more than spartan bathroom. Harry and I brought up two buckets of icy water from the well, which mother heated in inadequate pans on the new oil stove. Two pansful plus half a bucket of cold water were carried up the back stairs and sloshed into the full-length bath. This barely covered the bottom. By the time two more were heated the water was lukewarm and enthusiasm rapidly diminished. Harry was rushed in and out, and much to my disgust I shared his now tepid water. After use the bath had to be emptied by hand. There was no hole or plug. The water was scooped out by jug and two people tipped the remaining water into a bucket to carry down and empty in the garden. Bathing, from being a pleasurable end to one's day, became a wild extravagence to be indulged in weekly after much preparation and thought. How our parents regretted buying the largest bath, and only the thought of the difficulty of returning it to Tiverton restrained them from rushing out and changing it for a smaller model.

How lovely to go to bed by candlelight. The candles were kept in a cupboard in the butler's pantry, where father trimmed them and the oil lamps each morning. I had a deep copper candlestick with box of matches which I carried up to bed at night. We laid in a store of pottery 'pigs', which were filled earlier in the evening and covered with knitted covers. How snug to get into bed warmed by a plump 'pig' and to read by candlelight. Our bedrooms, though equipped with fireplaces, were, of course, unheated in wartime. Previously, they had doubtless been lit nightly by a housemaid. But they didn't seem cold that first winter because of the glow of the candle. After it had been blown out there was a smoky waxy smell which lingered in the air. Outside the rain continued its steady drenching deluge.

We were now more or less straight and settled in. The front, Regency part of the house was furnished, the back Elizabethan original left bare. Harry and I used the attics for roller skating when the rain became too heavy to venture out. The house was a long low white-washed house, standing half way up a hill about 500 feet high. It faced due south across the valley of an unnamed stream which flowed into the Batherm at Petton. Across the valley was Clayhanger on top of another hill, with hills rising beyond and beyond. There was a flagged verandah across the front of the house, which shaded the wide entrance hall and front rooms. On the west, leading out of the verandah, was a greenhouse with a small old vine, which yielded bunches of small sour grapes most years unless there was an exceptionally warm sunny summer. Under the roof was a wooden fretwork frill which continued all round the Regency house. From the wide hall a carved staircase curled round to a wide landing overlooking the front garden. A large wooden linen chest with a brass bowl holding flowers flanked by the brass Georgian candlesticks, stood in front of this window. On either side lay the main bedrooms facing south. Harry had a small room facing west and I was next door overlooking the courtyard. The last upstairs Regency room held the bath. There was a long gloomy corridor leading to the as yet unused Elizabethan wing.

The rooms were square and smallish with low ceilings. The drawing room looked larger than it really was owing to the smallness of the carpet. Facing the window was a large and beautiful carved mahogany sideboard, our only piece of furniture contemporary with the house. This glowed in the soft lights of the oil lamps and flickering firelight, surely the most flattering light for polished furniture. It had been in father's family since 1826. When he inherited it, there was in one of the drawers, a piece of paper reading 'Bought at Mrs. Robert's sale, Mevagissy, Dec. 27th. 1826.' It had been bought by his great grandfather. For generations father's family had been boat-builders in Mevagissy, known as 'Fishgissy' locally, famous at one time as one of the centres of the pilchard fishing. In the middle of the 19th. century, as the shoals of these fish became smaller owing to the pilchards leaving for fresh waters, just as the herrings leaving the Baltic contributed to the decline of Lubeck and the other Hanse towns at the end of the 15th. century, a number of families left Mevagissy for other parts of the country. Father's great grandfather Benjamin Drew settled in Liverpool in the early fifties of the 19th. century, and was killed by a hansom cab while setting his watch outside Oldfields watchmakers. His son, Captain Benjamin Drew was the master of the steamship Garonne, of the Charente Steamship Company, built in 1866. On 21st. May 1868 this ship was returning from Bordeaux to Liverpool carrying general cargo and sixteen passengers. Late the following night during fog, the ship struck the Bucks Rock outside Lamorna, and foundered in twenty minutes. Captain Drew was last seen on deck immediately prior to sinking. His body was found next day with a child clasped in his arms whom he had vainly endeavoured to save. He was buried in Mevagissy churchyard and his tomb can be seen today. He left a widow and two infant sons, one of whom was our grandfather. Many years later as a young man he went to Mevagissy and spoke to old fishermen who had been taught as children in his father's Sunday School class and still possessed Bibles given to them by him. We still have his sea chest made by him as a young man. When father went to Oxford, he filled it with books and it took four porters to carry it. Two of father's elder brothers went to sea, Uncle Harold, in a schooner whose captain in 1910 had long ringlets and golden ear-rings. In our generation one of our cousins is a Trinity House pilot, and now also his son. Our father, an historian, was the fourth son, but the only one to want the sideboard or chest. He in his turn as a young man went to Mevagissy and found cousins living there. We used the sideboard throughout our childhood as a toy cupboard.

Opposite the lounge was the dining room, also facing south, but with another window in the east wall looking out onto an enclosed vegetable garden. Overlooking the courtyard was a small dark study facing north. Beyond, downstairs, and along a passage was a large red and white tiled kitchen facing west and overlooking the courtyard. Later, when water was installed, a sink with a window above was made in the south-east corner, and in the thick walls a small round window was found, which must have been bricked over when the house was enlarged in 1823. Leading from the kitchen was a large flagged larder, to which Harry and I repaired on Sunday afternoons to slice pieces off the joint. North again was a huge damp stone-flagged scullery with a copper for clothes, the ten gallon tank for paraffin, an old fashioned mangle, and the table with the shame-faced primus. Later, when we were piped to the well, a wooden pump handle was installed here. Leading from this room up a short staircase was a maid's bedroom, looking north over the enclosed garden. For the first few months we used it as a nursery, and with the help of a stepladder, had our own private entrance to the garden.

Leading from the kitchen through a door were the back stairs. These led first to a locked room marked on the plan as 'Parish Room'. When we discovered the key and rushed eagerly in, it was found to be crammed with the left overs of 100 years of jumble sales, mouldering hassocks, original hymn books, forgotten curtains. Over the months we gradually burnt it in vast smouldering bonfires. Over this part of the house were also large and echoing attics, later used for some of our evacuees.

Beneath the front part of the house were large and damp cellars lined with racks for wine, reached by a door at the foot of the stairs. Shortly after our arrival a man arrived to convert them into an air raid shelter. As we were six miles from the nearest air raid siren, it was unlikely that we would have any warning of raids before the bombs fell. However, a second exit was made leading up onto the lawn in front of the verandah outside the lounge window. A small tumulus-shaped mound appeared with a wooden door at one end, which quickly became covered with grass. The only occasion when bombs fell in the parish was years later in mid-winter. The first one woke us up, the second, an hour later, a time bomb, sent us hurrying into the warm kitchen to spend the rest of the night huddled together under the table. No one thought of courting pneumonia in a water-logged dark cellar, which in any case, had not been 'blacked out.'

We arrived in Devon early in November 1939, and arrangements were made for us to start school in Taunton in January 1940. Although Taunton was over twenty miles away, the schools there were more accessible than those in Tiverton nine miles away. Harry was to go to King's College, and I to Bishop Fox's girls school. Meanwhile father taught us at home, a very satisfactory arrangement. We bought all the books required for me entering the first form, and settled down after breakfast every weekday in the dining room. Harry was still struggling with reading and writing, and he was provided with an old fashioned copy book and some sharpened pencils. Scratching noises punctuated with deep sighs came from his table. For the first time I really enjoyed learning. Father was a historian with a classical education who had been up at Oxford when both Greek and Greek New Testament were required for matriculation. We began the study of English history, literature and poetry that rainy winter, reading aloud alternately from books. Malory's Morte d'Arthur was the set English book, and reading it in the west country with a soft drizzly rain outside was an ideal setting. We read it through three times. It has stayed in my mind ever since as my real introduction to English literature. The poetry was taken from An Intermediate Poetry Book, selected and edited by Reed Moorhouse, with a picture of John Masefield Poet Laureate on the cover. The dedication was to the children who read this book, and began

> 'A little sun, a little rain, a soft wind blowing from the west,
> And woods and fields are sweet again,
> And warmth within the mountain's breast.'

Soft winds and rain with very little sun were our portion that winter. Every day we read and learned poetry from the selection, a catholic choice of Moorhouse, covering the whole range of English poetry from Edmund Spenser and Robert Mannyng of Brunne, to John Masefield and Robert Graves who were still living at that time. There was a great preponderance of late 16th. and 17th. century poets, including Shakespeare, John Milton, Andrew Marvell and Thomas Campion, and a fair sprinkling from the 18th. century. Many unknown 19th. and 20th. century poets were included, chiefly of interest to children. There was the usual patriotic verse and a few religious and traditional ones such as Ben Backstay. Every day I learnt a new poem or a few verses, and as a result of this early selection have preferred the Elizabethan and 17th. century poets ever since. I still remember the thrill of reading 'And Little Hunted Hares', by Shakespeare.

And Little Hunted Hares.

> But if thou needs wilt hunt, be ruled by me:
> Uncouple at the timerous flying hare,
> Or at the fox which lives by subtlety,
> Or at the roe which no encounter dare:
> Pursue these fearful creatures o'er the downs,
> And on thy well-breathe'd horse keep with thy hounds.

And when thou hast on foot the purblind hare,
Mark the poor wretch, to overshoot his troubles
How he outruns the wind, and with what care
He cranks and crosses with a thousand doubles:
The many musits through the which he goes
Are like a labyrinth to amaze his foes.

Sometime he runs among a flock of sheep,
To make the cunning hounds mistake their smell;
And sometimes where earth-delving conies keep,
To stop the loud pursuers in their yell;
And sometime sorteth with a herd of deer;
Danger deviseth shirts; wit waits on fear.

For there his smell with others being mingled,
The hot scent-snuffing hounds are driven to doubt,
Ceasing their clamorous cry till they have singled
With much ado the cold fault cleanly out:
Then do they spend their mouths: Echo replies,
As if another chase were in the skies.

By this, poor Wat, far off upon a hill,
Stands on his hinder legs with listening ear,
To hearken if his foes pursue him still:
Anon their loud alarums he doth hear;
And now his grief may be compared well
To one sore sick that hears the passing-bell.

Then shalt thou see the dew-bedaubed wretch
Turn, and return, indenting with the way;
Each envious briar his weary legs doth scratch,
Each shadow makes him stop, each murmur stay;
For misery is trodden on by many,
And being low never relieved by any.

Harry and I were ardent supporters of the wild animal against the human. In the country there was always someone blazing away at the rabbits, especially with the shortage of meat. Poachers were rife, and their traps lined the hedgerows and fields, every kind of trap from metal-toothed traps, which could have inflicted serious damage to human feet, to homemade nooses stretched over animal holes. We didn't realize at the time the human poverty of the countryside which drove men out to catch anything, however small, which could help to feed their families. I remember our horror when we discovered that boys got up before dawn to catch sleeping birds in the hedgerows to eat for breakfast. Years later in the Middle East I felt the same recoil on seeing the little pickled birds for sale.

I also learned by heart Edmund Spenser's 'The Hynde'. He and Shakespeare must have been amongst the earliest supporters of the hunted animal against the hunter, and certainly had our ardent support. Inconsistently we devoured huge helpings of rabbit and pigeon pie.

Father taught me English social history and a brief outline of European history in the last months of 1939. The emphasis was on the rightness of Britain, Nelson and Hardy being amongst his heroes. Years later in Paris, I was astonished at the reverence and homage paid to the dead Napoleon.

Little time was left for any other studies. Books were closed at lunch time and we fled into the fields and woods until dark every afternoon whatever the weather. Before leaving St. Helens I had had coaching in maths, particularly geometry and algebra in order to reach grammar school standard. But these were quickly forgotten and never regretted. We did a smattering of French and Latin, but no science of any kind. It was years before I caught up in maths, but in English and history and all the arts was well ahead.

The year drew to a close and we celebrated Christmas in our new home, the first Christmas of the war. In those far-off days we woke to feel a bulging stocking at our feet, tied on the end of the bed on Christmas Eve. We opened them together, long before anyone else was up. They were filled with small wooden toys, painted dollshouse dolls and furniture, lead animals for the farm, lead soldiers, pencils, tiny notebooks, a handful of nuts, and in the toe a tangerine and a new penny from the bank. How we enjoyed the feel of the stocking, and savouring each item. Then after breakfast to Church to sing the carols of Christmas. After lunch we had our presents. Always a book from our parents, and there would be parcels from the aunts, mother's sisters, Aunt Trudy in the Naafi in the Isle of Man, and Aunt Nancy in Bolton - useful presents of clothes from her, something homemade from Trudy. And postal-orders for half a crown from father's sisters. Anything over sixpence had to be saved, so we only had a brief look at these riches, before they were put carefully away to take to the post office. In the darkening afternoon we went a long walk with father while mother made the tea. Then down to our books by the fire as the year ebbed away.

Timmy and Tithe Barn.

Ruined cottage across road.

Miss Franklin, Nancy, June
Hugh and Harry.

Watersplash.

Chapter 3.   THE GARDEN AND GLEBE

The Hills of Youth

Once, on the far blue hills,
Alone with the pine and the cloud, in those high still places;
Alone with a whisper of ferns and a chuckle of rills,
And the peat-brown pools that mirrored the angels' faces,
Pools that mirrored the wood-pigeon's grey-blue feather,
And all my thistledown dreams as they drifted along;
Once, oh, once, on the hills, thro' the red-bloomed heather
I followed an elfin song.
                    Alfred Noyes

In the west of England the day after Christmas is dedicated to the shooting of wild animals. We had all been invited to join the shoot at Nutcombe Manor, a mile away across the fields. We set out eagerly after breakfast in a light cool drizzle which steadily increased all day, until we returned drenched through in the early evening. All the local farmers were present with their families, and the shoot began in earnest about eleven. Father did not shoot and was there in his pastoral capacity. It was an opportunity for him to meet parishioners whom he had not yet met. Mother was soon chatting away under the inadequate shelter of a large tree. Harry and I roamed round with the sportsmen blazing away at the rabbits. It was largely a bag of rabbits. No game birds were reared in the woods during the war. Mr. Williams, who owned Nutcombe Manor at that time, was a farmer who concentrated chiefly on cattle and sheep, and only once a year organized a shoot. We were allowed to shoot by one farmer, and were glad to miss. The slaughter seemed terrific to us, and reminded us of an occasion in Cambridge when we had seen two thousand pheasants shot in the Gog-ma-Gog hills. The rabbits were laid out in dozens and we all ate rabbit for what seemed like weeks to come.

Lunch was served informally. Wartime restrictions were in force and we brought our own sandwiches, beer being provided for the men and sherry for the women. We ate our lunch in the great hall of the house, which was decorated with plaster carvings round the mantlepiece and the ceiling. The huge smouldering log on the fire did little to warm the December day although the clothes of those near enough began to steam gently. The house dated from about 1600, and was built on an older site which was still visible in the ground plan of the house. It was a small manor house set in neglected gardens, and surrounded by fields and woods. The original house had been owned by the Nutcombe's who had rebuilt it in 1600; but either the family died out, or they left shortly afterwards. The Lords of the Manor after them were named Bluett, and their family owned the house until the early years of this century. Mr. Williams left while we were there, and sold the estate to a grand-daughter of Lord Carnarvon of Pixhill Park, Dulverton, a Roman Catholic.

There was an estate at Nutcombe in the 11th. and 12th. centuries when the property was owned by the Knights' Templars. No trace of them remained, no ruined chapel or barn, or even fishpond. Their manor was probably on the same site, and must have been in ruins when the Nutcome's rebuilt the house. Doubtless some of the early stones were incorporated in the house. There seemed no remains of the Templars either physically in the landscape, or in folklore, and no memorial remained of them in the church. They had gone as though they had never been. Harry and I were of a romantic turn of mind and our heads were filled with King Arthur and his knights. We pictured these knights dressed in their robes with black crosses, walking up through the woods to church. It was always in the evening we imagined them, with a light mist along the forest glades as they walked silently in twos through the gloaming. They were going to spend the night in vigil in the church, their swords and helmets beside them in readiness, before setting off next day for the Holy Land. Very satisfactory reminiscences, unhampered by any known inconvenient facts.

After lunch the shooting began again, and the rain increased in heaviness. We left in a torrential downpour in the late afternoon, with darkness already gathering.

The date of the original rectory on the site where we lived was not known, but was probably Tudor. Our house had been rebuilt on the same site in 1823 at a cost of £1,000. A stone wall continued the house on the west and south, making a courtyard at the back of the house. The courtyard was overlooked by the west-facing rooms of the Elizabethan house and the north-facing study and bedrooms of the Regency house. Looking at the wing from the yard, there was an arched window from the backstairs landing with stained glass panes, still in existence today. This was flanked by bedroom windows. Above were the attics, with shaggy eyebrows of slate. The kitchen and scullery looked out into the yard and the back door opened this way. A door in the west wall led into the yard from the back drive and a stone flagged path led to the back door. In the middle was a round bed containing a cherry tree which bore copious fruit all the years we were there. Perhaps the birds were kinder in those days, but we always seemed to have a good crop of luscious fruit. Below the walls were flower beds, and under the study windows bushes of honesty. The flagged path was lined with large fossils. Along the west wall were sheds. The north wall was old and wide and steps led up to a gate in the wall which led into an enclosed garden, partly walled and partly surrounded by a high hedge. This wall was covered in June with wild strawberry plants and we often picked several dishes. On the side facing the garden was a climbing rose, the old fashioned pink Albertine. Even in winter the courtyard was a warm place to sit if the sun was shining, the white painted walls of the house reflecting the light. Immediately to the right on entering the courtyard was a woodshed which ran along the width of the house, and backed on to the greenhouse. It was huge and filled with a lovely smell of sawn wood. After the trees had been felled, it was full of branches waiting to be sawn up. There was a trestle to rest logs on while sawing, and hanging on the whitewashed walls were various saws and billhooks.

The house was approached by two long winding drives, named on the plan of the house, the coach and carriage drives. Coming from the village at the foot of the hill, one crossed the stream and entered the lower carriage drive, by an old wooden gate across the drive on which we swung. At the foot of the drive was a small wood, and an avenue of trees lined the gravelled path. On the left, the trees were on a bank which sloped abruptly to the road out of sight below. On the right, behind the trees was a fence beyond which was one of the glebe meadows. The drive swept round to the right in front of the house branching to enclose a large circular flower bed in front of the front door. This was filled with roses surrounded by a ring of grass. Beyond the bed the drive turned into a path leading into the fields by a swing gate. Leaving this drive on the right and going on up the hill one could see the house at the end of the drive for a few yards before the bank steepened abruptly and the trees towered above the road. About half way up the hill was the well which was later enclosed with an oak door. The coach drive led into the garden between steep banks. On the left was a bank covered with young trees, and on the right, the wooded bank which flanked the road. This drive forked right to join the carriage drive and straight on to a flagged path in front of imposing outbuildings. There was stabling for several horses and a garage which held two cars. Above was a loft and at the side, rooms for a groom or coachman, one room above the other with windows looking south into the garden. We played endlessly here on wet days during the first few months. The lower room we used as a museum, starting with a shelf of large fossils collected from the courtyard. We added multi-striped rocks from the quarries, birds nests, pressed flowers and grasses, butterflies and bones. The bones and teeth we picked up in fields and were probably from sheep. We tried once to dry all the bones of a chicken (after consumption of the bird), and to fit them together again into a skeleton, but it wasn't successful, and they were lumped together in a box labelled 'foul's bones'. Foul bones would have been nearer the mark when we discovered that the box was the source of a peculiar smell which lingered in the room.

The room above the museum was grandly termed 'The Russian Room'. Our maternal grandmother had spent some years in Russia as a young girl in the 1890's, where her father and grandfather had been textile engineers in what was then St. Petersburg. Her family had been in Russia since the 1830's, but had always returned to England to marry. We never tired of hearing tales of old Russia which our mother had heard in her own childhood. Romantic tales of frozen rivers and dark forests, and windswept plains, tales of snuggling in furs on sledges drawn by ponies with flat wooden snow shoes, whilst wolves howled behind in packs and peered with their bloodshot eyes between the trees. It sent cold shivers down our own spines to hear them. Our grandfather had travelled across Europe to fetch his bride without a passport, taking a week over the journey. The rest of the family remained in Russia until 1914, when some managed to return. The rest were forced to flee in 1917, and to leave all that they possessed behind. In the early 1920's a cousin of mother's returned and found their trunks untouched, and was able to bring personal belongings home. His dog was still there and rushed to him, eyes streaming with tears, but he was forced once again to leave him behind.

In our early childhood, we knew our 'Russian' great grandfather who lived to be 90, and his children our great aunts and uncles, who often pretended they had forgotten how to speak English. Grandmother used to sing Russian songs and mother also knew some. She had inherited a painted wooden table in bright reds and blues and golds which we had in the centre of the room. The only other Russian item was an old wooden doll with seven smaller dolls inside. Great grandfather as a boy of 12 had been in Russia when the serfs were freed in 1862, and never forget the sight of their joy at freedom, although perforce most of them remained on the great estates, but as free and paid workers.

Beyond the coachhouse the drive petered out into a path which led past a large run where we kept hens. This was on one side of a flagged yard much overgrown with grass which had a large tithe barn in the middle, antedating the house by about 100 years. The tithe barn was painted white like the house. It had a steeply sloping tiled roof. On the south side was a door high in the wall which led to a loft where hay and corn had previously been stored. On the east was the main entrance, leading into a large white washed room. The tithes had been commuted in 1840 for £244, which was invested to augment the living. The barn was in use as a village hall. It had been refloored with wooden planks and was heated by a large circular coal stove. There were large hanging oil lamps of brass with white china shades. These could be lowered by chains for filling and lighting.

During the war the hall was used for entertainment in the evenings and occasionally by the Home Guard. In those days socials as well as dances were popular. Once a year a variety show was staged by the village, songs and recitations and short sketches being the chief items. The dances were real country affairs, the barn dance still being the most popular, and a lot of old country dances were still in use. Father among his many other duties was responsible for filling and lighting the oil lamps, and lighting the ancient black stove, and putting up the blackout. The blackout was made of hardboard cut to fit the windows exactly, and painted black. These were easy to fit and clipped neatly into place.

One spring evening in 1941 there was to be a dance in the barn. As he had to attend a confirmation a few miles away during the afternoon with some of the children, father filled the lamps and lighted the stove in the morning. The stove was awkward and wouldn't light. The wind must have been in the wrong direction and all it would do was smoulder and smoke. As time was passing quickly, he fetched some paraffin and poured in a liberal amount. No result, except a puff of acrid smoke. He poured in some more and peered into the stove. Whoosh, the whole lot burst into flames and a flame shot upwards enveloping his face and singeing his hair. Half blinded and choking with the fumes he stumbled into the house. Mother bathed his face with olive oil and acriflavin ointment. This turned his face bright yellow. With no eyebrows and frizzled hair he looked an alarming sight. However, quite undaunted he set off with his small group of children to the confirmation. The few clergy present at the confirmation sat in the choir, and father sat next to the oldest member of the deanery, a rector then in his 90th. year. He wore Victorian clothes, and being almost stone deaf, carried a large antique ear trumpet. Curzon, the Lord Bishop of Exeter, was rather taken aback by the appearance in the choir of this ancient sitting next to what appeared to be a Chinese priest. Word had travelled quickly round the village and more than usual turned up at the dance that evening.

Although the garden was some three and a half acres in extent, it was smaller than it had formerly been. Looking from the front door there was a series of terraces to the little wood at the foot of the drive. The top terrace was the drive and a strip of lawn which fell steeply to a lawn about the size of a tennis court. This sloped steeply to what was then the glebe meadow. At the foot of the slope was a fence. The meadow in turn gave way to a bank above the stream. Opposite the house at the foot of the terraces the stream had been deepened and widened to form a small ornamental lake. In the middle was an island with a weeping willow tree. A perfect hide-out, and one constantly in use. We used a dilapidated, leaking punt to reach it as the pond was too deep for our wellingtons.

To the east of the house was a thick high hedge with a gate leading into the enclosed garden. This garden flanked the east and north sides of the house, and was L-shaped. There were paths between the beds and the whole of this garden, well over an acre in extent was devoted to fruit and vegetables, planted and tended by father who is a keen gardener. He was helped rather erratically by a boy from the village and sundry evacuees who were mainly from towns. In the north-west corner of the vegetable garden, opposite the gate from the courtyard, was a terrace, with a flight of stone steps leading up to a tiny lawn. Harry and I took this as our own garden and called it the 'pleasaunce'. The tiny wall surrounding it we grandly called the 'ha ha'. Below this we had our own beds, which we kept in a desultory manner. The first few months we had direct access to the house by means of a stepladder to the nursery window which faced north over this garden. To the west of the house at the top of the drive, was a large lawn called the croquet lawn, on which we played various games.

There was no orchard in the garden as we had it. In the Victorian larger garden, the orchard was in the field overlooking the stream beyond the glebe meadow. The orchard was in the glebe but was rented to a farmer, and although we regarded it as rightly ours we couldn't actually pick the fruit into baskets, but had to be content with a few windfalls.

The garden was surrounded by forty acres of glebe, all under pasture. The meadow east and south of the house was entered by a gate from the garden and ran down to the stream. In the summer of 1940 Mrs. Mowat, the wife of father's old tutor at Oxford, then Professor of History at Bristol University, painted the house from this meadow. She set up a wooden easel and painted in water colours. I set up my blackboard and also painted the house. We have Mrs. Mowat's delightful painting hung in our cottage today some sixty miles away in Dorset. While she was painting it I had time to do two paintings. Having completed the house in bolder colours than hers, I turned my board round and painted the village. Seen from the meadow it was up a steep hill. At the top was a yellow-washed farmhouse and a large black barn. A yellow barn with a flight of steps leading up to an open door lay behind. Across the yard was another farm of red brick, and beyond again was the greystone church with its tall Devon tower.

Beyond this meadow was another in which lay the orchard and a small copse. This was known as the Lynches. The small field beyond had a larger wood. We called it quarry wood because of the large quarry in the middle. We often played there and brought loads of stone home with us for the museum, shiny striped stones of many colours easily broken off from the quarry face. The bottom of this field running along the stream was marked on the map 'No man's bottom'.

Beyond the tithe barn was the Barn Meadow. Here in January 1940 three large oak trees were felled with a might crash. We played for weeks in their branches before they were cut up for timber. The smaller branches were ours for firewood. The main trunks were for some reason I no longer remember blown up by dynamite at the end of February.

During this first winter we spent every day exploring until the term started and we had to limit our activities to the weekends, as it was dark after school. We chiefly loved the streams and waded up stream for hours exploring the various small tributaries and breaking down the overhanging branches with a bill hook if we could sneak one away unseen. We both had fairly large clasp knives which we were always cutting ourselves with. We used to come home soaked and muddy. Only a few yards upstream it suddenly deepened and our wellingtons tightened with the pressure of water, then loosened suddenly as it rushed over the top and there was a squelchy muddy feel about the toes. Then, when the water shallowed we precariously balanced on alternate feet emtying them out. We always wore the same matted damp socks inside our wellingtons, which we kept pushed down inside the toe at home so that mother should not know we had got our feet wet yet again. I don't ever remember putting on dry wellingtons except when they were new. Sometimes we pushed wads of newspaper into the feet which dried them slightly. Always we had dark muddly rims round our legs below the knee where the edge of the wellington rubbed. The bottoms of our gaberdines were also perpetually damp and muddy. But we were happy and never at a loss for anything to do. In the middle of January snow fell and we skated on the ice of the pond. But alas, Harry started school on 13th. and it was not nearly so much fun alone. I went to school on 16th. and our first carefree months were over.

Chapter 4.   CALLERS

Cranford: Our Society by Mrs. Gaskell

'There were rules and regulations for visiting and calls; and they were announced to any young people who might be staying in the town, with all the solemnity with which the old Manx laws were read once a year on the Tinwald Mount ...

'After they had called: 'It is the third day; I dare say your mamma has told you, my dear, never to let more than three days elapse between receiving a call and returning it; and also, that you are never to stay longer than a quarter of an hour .... You must keep thinking about the time, my dear, and not allow yourself to forget it in conversation.

As everybody had this rule in their minds, whether they received or paid a call, of course no absorbing subject was ever spoken about. We kept ourselves to short sentences of small talk, and were punctual to our time.'

Until the outbreak of war in 1939 calling was still practised in England as was so well described by Elizabeth Gaskell and Jane Austen in their novels. In country districts the wives of gentry and professional people called on each other and returned the calls. The calling took place in the afternoons after a suitable interval had elapsed since lunch, and before it was time to return home for afternoon tea. It was a pleasant way of filling the afternoon, and ensured that there was a close-knit group of people all over the country who knew each other and followed a similar way of life. When a newcomer came to a country district, the local people for perhaps five to seven miles round about, depending on the population density, called. It was probably the distance which could be easily covered by a pony trap until the first World War. If the lady was not at home, a card would be left and the caller would call again if she had not already met her. If she already knew her the card would be sufficient and she would await a return call. When someone had called or left a card, after a few weeks the call would be returned and the ball started rolling. One was accepted in the new society and there was a new face to be seen. Tea might be offered the caller or a formal invitation extended for this meal.

From earliest childhood I remember mother's small leather case where she kept her cards. In the hall we kept a brass plate where cards were left by people calling, and when she called in her turn, she left a card.

In the sparsely populated countryside of north Devon a newcomer was a great treat, and although it was wartime it was still the 'phoney war, and social conditions had not yet radically altered. We had a fairly wide variety of callers. The local clergy and their wives came to see us, far more of them than there are now. Until the war it was still quite usual for there to be a rector or vicar in a tiny village or hamlet of less than five hundred people, living in vast old houses near the church. Now with the shortage of clergy, greater mobility and vastly changed living conditions, most of the small parishes are joined up. Father was the last resident rector of Clayhanger. which was joined to Huntsham after his departure. Now all the small villages are served from Bampton and the rectories sold. The rector of Huntsham had a gloomy old Victorian rectory of vast size. His patron was his neighbour, Colonel Acland-Troyte of Huntsham Court, the M.P. for Tiverton for many years. One of his ancestors in the 1850's had been both patron and incumbent, a squireson, one of the unique features of the Church of England. A squireson was both Lord of the Manor and Rector of the parish, temporal and spiritual lord. Colonel Acland-Troyte and his wife called, and also Mr. and Mrs. Fleetwood-Hesketh of Holcombe Rogus Court, members of a Lancashire family with land round Southport and Fleetwood. In the 1850's the Bluett's had been Lords of the Manor there, relations of those at Nutcombe Manor.

The Court at Holcombe Rogus exerted a great fascination on Harry and me as it was reputed to be haunted. We listened spellbound to the tales the callers told us. They lived there all alone with their children grown and gone. Often in the evening they would hear a distant bell ring, and then footsteps slowly walk in the room above them, followed by a clanking bell and chain. There was one room where nothing apparently happened, but there was such an unhappy feeling in it that no one would sleep there, a small bedroom, one of the family rooms not a servant's room. Later in the war soldiers were billetted on the court, and some of the young soldiers given the room to sleep in. After the first night they flatly refused to sleep there again, but could give no reason. A few months later during repairs to the house, in the wall of the room was found the skeleton of a murdered young woman and a baby. The bodies were buried by the rector, and the haunting ceased.

One caller amused us. I was home from school with a mild attack of German measles when two ladies arrived to call. They had both just recovered from German measles themselves, but on learning that I was infected, flatly refused to come into the house, and paid their call on the verandah in a mad March gale.

As we had no car it was difficult for mother to return many calls. She did return some in a hired car, and some on foot, but after mid-1940 calling almost ceased. Some twenty years later when I was married and living in Baghdad, to my surprise my mother-in-law sent me a carved ivory card case with a note saying 'I expect people still call in Baghdad'. My mother-in-law was right, the custom still prevailed abroad amongst English people. I think that to a certain degree people still call in remote country districts of England, but not to the same extent as was practised before the war.

Two of our earliest visitors were Mr. and Mrs. Parsons of Sampford Peverell. They were the houseparents of the Boniface Home for boys run by the Waifs and Strays (now the Church of England Childrens Society). They lived in a large rambling old house in Sampford Peverell some seven miles away. They were a delightful warm hearted couple, devoted to the twenty or so boys in their care. We went over there for tea shortly after, a vast childrens' tea of plenty of bread and butter and jam and wedges of slab cake. They had a large vegetable garden, and were anxious to sell their produce to augment the frugal income from the society. Later in the war when we had our evacuees Mr. Parsons used to come over with twelve pounds of tomatoes at a time. When we were awaiting the arrival of the evacuees he lent us many essentials until we were able to obtain them ourselves. The boys made articles of wood and stools with canework seats which we bought periodically. We still have two 3-legged milking stools made by them.

In Clayhanger there was no village shop. There was a sub-post office, run from a tiny front room of a small cottage. This sold only post office goods, some stationery and string. Everything else had to come from the nearest small towns, Wiveliscombe in Somerset, or Bampton in Devon, both five miles away. Neither would seem far today, but it was quite a feat to shop in either. It was two miles to Venn Cross Station, where one could get trains to Wiveliscombe, the next station towards Taunton. But there would be a long wait there to return. To get to Bampton would involve changing at Morebath Junction Halt, and would take the best part of the day. However, there was no need to shop in person. The village was excellently served by shops which called. They came from a great variety of places near and far, at various times.

Our grocer was D. W. Dunsford of Tiverton, who called every other week. We got all our groceries from him, and when he arrived with the order mother would give him the next order. As the war progressed the order got simpler, as one could only order the amount of goods one was entitled to on ones ration card, and foreign goods virtually disappeared from the menu. The fishmonger came from Wellington, about eighteen miles away in Somerset. We never discovered his name. He came in a plain van and would only accept cash, no cheques, and remained anonymous. Even if we wished to do so, it would have been almost impossible to reach Wellington to shop in person. He was a useful caller as he provided sausages and bananas as well as fish. The bananas disappeared towards the end of 1940. He delivered on a Thursday morning and we ate the fish on Friday for lunch.

The butcher was closer, from Hockworthy, south of us some six or seven miles along a winding lane. He came twice a week with meat and eggs. Often he had duck eggs which were a great boon, as they were not affected by rationing, and were good for scrambled eggs and cakes. The market gardener called every week with vegetables and fruit he grew himself on a small holding near Wiveliscombe. The baker came twice a week from Ashbrittle five miles away. Sometimes we would walk there and always stopped at his shop for warm floury loaves and large soft currant buns. In the early months we used to spread the buns thick with jam and cream, and then eat them toasted for breakfast the next day.

A Mr. Mason came once a month selling paraffin, furniture and china. The furniture and china were a hopeful sideline, as it was mostly paraffin he sold. During the winter months when the school was with us we used fifty gallons a month. Just before they arrived mother bought a large quantity of plain china from him, breakfast, dinner and tea sets, thirty of everything, a useful order.

If one had forgotten anything useful one could usually depend on a man from Petton who came daily with newspapers and had a travelling shop, which sold virtually everything in small quantities.

The laundry came from Taunton weekly. The only things we sent were sheets, pillowcases and large towels, of which we had huge numbers when the school was with us. They used to be packed in a large old-fashioned wickerwork laundry basket. We had two of these, one packed with the dirty linen and one at the laundry waiting to return with the clean. Winnie Tucker who came to help several mornings a week used to take our personal washing and the small towels home with her. During term time she often had thirty to thirty-five peoples' washing to do, a truly noble war work. I remember toiling up the hill with huge bundles to the house where she lived with her mother at the other end of the village.

A less popular visitor was Dr. Morgan from Bampton. He would give us prescriptions which had to be made up by the chemist in Wiveliscombe. occasionally if there was no train someone would cycle over there. Early in the war we went to a travelling dentist whom we visited when he came to Wiveliscombe. Later in the war he blew off part of his hand with a grenade when in the Home Guard, which temporarily finished his career, and then we went to Mr. Setterington in Taunton.

In the west of England today there are many small places without a village shop, and meat, groceries and vegetables and bread are still delivered by travelling shops, the owners of which also bring that most indispensable item, the news, which circulates much faster by word of mouth than by post these days.

Chapter 5.   SCHOOL

Childish Recollections

> I cannot but remember such things were,
> And were most dear to me.
>
> Scenes of my youth, developed, crowd to view,
> To which I long have bade a last adieu!
> Seats of delight, inspiring youthful themes;
> Friends lost to me for aye, except in dreams.
>   Lord Byron.

On 16th. January 1940 I started school in the first form of Bishop Fox's Girls' School in Taunton. This entailed a fairly considerable amount of travelling to and fro each day. In those days it wasn't considered necessary to transport children to and from their homes by bus after they reached the age of eleven. There was no primary school in Clayhanger, and the children aged 5 - 14 were collected by bus and taken to Shillingford School. During the years we were there none passed the 11 plus examination, so I was the only one going to a grammar school from the village. The school for the area was in Tiverton, quite inaccessible in wartime. As I went to school in Somerset an extra £1 per term was charged in fees!

The train left Venn Cross at 8.05 from Venn Cross, and often I was the only passenger as far as Wiveliscombe, where a crowd of school children and workers got on. That first winter our parents hired a car to take Harry and me to the station in the morning as he was only eight and it was about two miles. The car was owned and driven by Mr. Hannam, who lived in the hamlet of Waterrow, half way to Wiveliscombe. He was meant to call for us at 7.45, but he specialized in catching the train by a hairsbreadth, and would often arrive at eight. There was fortunately no need to worry about meeting any other traffic along the one way lane that led to Venn Cross, as the possibility in wartime was remote. There were restrictions on the use of petrol and only farmers had it for their tractors and landrovers. We used to rush along chatting about adventure stories. Hannam was devoted to G. A. Henty, and would recount his historical adventures as we went along. He was obviously convinced that they were true, and so were we. I had just begun to read John Buchan, and we used to swop books. When we reached the top of the hill, there would be the train puffing down the valley or actually whistling as we entered the station. The car more or less left the road as it hurtled round the corners and down the hill. 'Hurry, Hannam, hurry, hurry', we cried clinging for dear life to the seats ready to dash out as we scorched to a stop. If he saw us the driver would wait as we rushed across the line.

It was always nerve-racking driving with Hannam, although we almost always caught the train. If we missed it, the next train was at eleven, a three hour wait. Once we missed it and went hurtling on to Wiveliscombe. The road left the railway beyond Waterrow, and took a wide detour to avoid a steep hill which the train ran through in a tunnel, so the road was some two miles further, and very winding and steep. We rushed over the miles, our hearts in our mouths as we went down the knife edged hairpin bend just before the village. We caught the train that time, but later on I waited more than once at Wiveliscombe for the next one. Our parents always ordered Hannam's services by letter and not telephone. Telephone was not used so lightly in those days for other than local calls, and letters were always delivered the next day. He used to write back confirming the booking and ending 'With anticipatory thanks' before his signature.

On reaching Taunton we separated and walked a mile or so to our respective schools. In the evenings we did our homework at school before catching the train home at 5.30 p.m. We walked home from the station, arriving soon after seven that first winter, before the train began to be seriously delayed by raids in London.

After half term Harry went as a weekly boarder to Taunton as the journey was much too tiring for an eight year old, and I went alone. Hannam continued to take me and I walked back in the evening with a torch. As a consequence of all those early walks I have never been afraid of the country dark. It was about two miles by the road, uphill half way then a long slope down. In daylight there was a short cut across two fields.

After Easter 1940 Hannam stopped taking me and I walked both ways to the station. Every morning I had breakfast in the nice warm kitchen at seven, and then left for school at half past. The house was about 550 feet above sea level on the side of Combe Downs which rose above us to a height of 800 feet. Turning right outside the drive, the road went uphill about a mile, a winding road between high banks topped with trees. There was a track off to the left to a farm perched high above the road. The road did not go continuously uphill, but dipped and turned and twisted about, 'up along down along'. In a damp hollow was Well Hayes farm surrounded by cider apple orchards. The fields round the house were very heavy and wet and there was thick Devon mud round the gateways. Beyond the farm the road rose steeply. At the top of the hill a track came in from the left

On the verandah – Miss Franklin and the infants.

Mother and father.

Nancy, June and father.

leading back to the farm on the hill, and the road ran along the top of the hill before sharply dropping to the railway which ran along the foot of the valley between Combe Downs and Shute Hill, which rose in the distance to over 900 feet. There was a short cut across two fields which cut off a good half mile, although one really needed wellingtons to use it most of the year. It ran past a farmhouse, and often in spring there would be a tame lamb or two who came running up to butt against one hopefully for food.

I used to dream along with my satchel on my back, strolling along the lanes as it grew lighter and lighter. Mostly I was Richard Hannay in pursuit of German agents, and quite often did not use the road at all but crept along the top of the high banks or just inside the fields, stalking along, and occasionally dashing across the road to a more convenient field. Often at the top of Well Hayes hill I would hear the train and then dash full pelt down the hill and across the fields. Fortunately I was the only one to get on at Venn Cross, and as long as I was not too late, the driver waited, puffing impatiently in the station. Then I would sink exhausted into the seat as we rushed snorting into the tunnel. There were two tunnels and a long high viaduct over the Tone valley at Waterrow, with lovely wooded views up to Heydon Hill. At Wiveliscombe several school children got on, some older girls from my school, as the town is in Somerset. I travelled the farthest distance each day to school out of the 800 or so pupils. We were fairly quiet in the mornings as we were usually all busy finishing off our homework. It was the evenings which were noisy. The girls who caught the train stayed in school until five and did homework there before going to catch the train. We often had to wait a long time at the station as the war progressed. Fortunately it was warm. There was always a huge coal fire in the waiting room, and we toasted ourselves well while we waited. Outside in the winter it would be dark and the waiting room was blacked out. The wait often seemed endless for the London train. Our own train, the Barnstable train, was already waiting in its siding, but we never sat in it in the dark until it was ready to go. When the express rushed in we rushed out to our train and piled in hoping to keep the carriage free of grown-ups. As soon as the train left we got up into the rack for the rest of the journey, and only our satchels and books travelled on the seats, except at stations which would see us decorously seated as though butter wouldn't melt in our mouths. We had to keep the blinds down because of the blackout regulations and the lights were painted purple so it was a very dim journey, quite impossible to read. We larked about and periodically the guard would come along to quell the noise. 'Now, now, what's all this about' he'd say, and quiet would reign for a few minutes.

Although the train was often delayed, the war didn't impinge with any sense of reality until the time of Dunkirk. Our parents were anxiously glued to the wireless those days when our army was falling back on the coast of France, and France was capitulating to the Germans. Then the little ships fetched them home, and one evening when we came from school, the whole platform was covered with sleeping worn-out soldiers, bristly about the chin, with no luggage. Just in their worn battledress they lay lost to the world. They seemed to be there for days, and it brought the war very close. My godfather, an army chaplain, stayed on the beaches of Dunkirk with the men who couldn't be saved in time, and spent five years a prisoner of war in Germany.

Often I was away from home from 7.30 in the morning until eight or nine at night when the train was very late. The earliest I could get home was six thirty if the train was on time, as it was a good half hour's walk from the station home. Nowadays such conditions would seem intolerable for children, but we took it quite for granted and grew up healthy and strong. Small children of five would walk a couple of miles from a lonely farm for the school bus. We recovered over the weekend from any lack of sleep.

I walked to and from the station every day from the summer of 1940 until my fifteenth birthday in 1943. Then I had a longed for bicycle, a black-painted wartime BSA, to conform to the blackout regulations. On this vehicle the front light was practically blacked out, only a tiny square allowing out the light. However, it cut down the time of the journey although I never managed to cycle right up Well Hayes hill. I cut the journey even finer, although I was no longer Richard Hannay, but usually fleeing from some German agent who had similar transport. There was still the last minute rush for the train from the top of the hill. Once when I missed it I cycled on to Wiveliscombe, missed it there and went on. It was a fine sunny day, and I rode to Taunton, seeing a slightly different view of the countryside than from the train. Milverton was a lovely Georgian village and I looked round the church and bought some broken biscuits to fortify myself. Then the long downhill ride to the Somerset plain through Norton Fitzwarren and past Taunton School, whose playing fields joined ours. I arrived eventually at 11.30, beating the second train by half an hour. This was not fully appreciated by the staff, who often seemed lacking in a sense of humour. None of them had to cope with anything like that journey each day. In the evening I rode home again, leaving straight after school, and was home long before I would have been by train, to the surprise of our parents. They could hardly believe I'd cycled over fifty miles that day, as neither of them ever mounted a bicycle. It was the only time I did it and for a few weeks caught the train in comfort.

During the war there were two or three major crashes at Norton Fitzwarren, the first on 4th. November 1940, when the wreckage was strewn all over the line with carriages flung over, and the two engines smashed together. Our train arrived immediately after one smash, and they were carrying the bodies out of the wreckage. All had quite a high loss of life, and serious injury. Nowadays rail travel seems to have become much safer.

In January 1940 I entered one of the first forms of which there were three. It seemed an enormous school, and was the largest I ever attended, there being three parallel forms up the school as far as the sixth. The first form were far ahead of me in most subjects, especially maths, of which I knew virtually nothing of value apart from the tables. But in English and History I had a far greater general knowledge thanks to father. Everyone else had been there one more term and had already made friends, and from the first I hated this school. The school I had started in at five was in a large old family house and was warm and friendly with small classes. Bishop Fox's School was in brand new buildings built on a lavish scale. The school was built round two courtyards with the hall and offices across the front, and the cloakrooms, laboratories, and the domestic science and art block across the back. Joining these blocks was the gymnasium in the middle flanked by two grass grown courtyards, then classrooms either side. The classrooms were very modern with either side of glass, and only the front and back were walls. It was more or less impossible to heat in wartime, and the whole of each winter, life was a misery from nine to five, and feet and hands were swollen with chilblains. The first winter my brain was also chilled with cold and misery at school. The maths and French were over my head, and the English and history were so boring as I had already covered all the ground with father. Needlework took up one afternoon a week and we were making cookery aprons. Everything was done by hand and not dashed off on the machine as we would have done in half the time at home. The whole of the first term was spent sewing, unpicking and resewing a run and fell seam. The material was grimy and lank at the end of the term, spattered with drops of blood from pricked fingers. For years I have made my own clothes, and never once have had to do a run and fell seam again, although it is imprinted on my memory for life. The only thing at which I excelled at first was gym, which we did three times a week. The gym was well fitted out with wonderful equipment, and fun. But the other two afternoons were spent on an icy field at hockey and netball, with neither of which I had any acquaintance. The others had been initiated the previous term, and hared up and down waving their sticks wildly in all directions. Our ankles used to be black and blue at the end of the afternoons when we hobbled back inside.

September 1940 found me still in form one, and the second year in that form was even worse. The English and history repeated ad nauseum drove me to despair, and although I now understood dimly the French and maths. it seemed pointless to repeat everything again. I did so badly at the end of the year that not surprisingly I was put in 2c. 2a did classics, 2b science and 2c domestic science. Of everything taught I loathed domestic science more than any other. Father tried to insist on me being put in the classics form, but to no avail. Years later when I went to the university I had to spend an extra year just learning Latin, because of not having had the opportunity at a school which actually taught it.

In the second form, apart from needlework we also did cookery and housekeeping, all boring, and all bearing little relation to the actual realities of housekeeping at home. In cookery we learned to cook on electric stoves. i hadn't occurred to the mid-twentieth century education authorities to provide a coal range or oil stove, in spite of the fact that this school served a radius of twenty miles round Taunton, and none of the remote village or hamlets were reached by the electric cable. We were allowed to take home the food we had cooked. The first term we made a milky rice pudding which I carried hopefully home in the dark for two miles. it kept slopping about all over the place, and my gaberdene and shoes were covered with splashes of milk. There was a small pool in the bottom of the dish with some skin to eat cold for supper. At the end of term I got my first A in any subject for a bread and butter pudding. It looked and smelt delicious, and I bore it proudly home. Heated up it was uneatable, and mother swore I'd put starch and not sugar in it. Quite likely. Fortunately no one had tasted it at school. It was judged solely on its mouth-watering appearance.

During the second year at long last I finished my apron. it had two pockets in the front and a panel of embroidery. Much too good to wear for cooking, especially after the hours spent producing it. It should really have been framed. I never liked it and soon mislaid it, and wore a much more useful overall provided by mother.

One thing which the whole school did which was interesting in the needlework line was a tapestry of Bishop Fox for the cathedral at Wells. The Friends of Wells Cathedral in the 1930's decided to commemorate in tapestry some of the bishops from its foundation in 909 to the present day. Each tapestry is similar. In the middle is a shield with the arms of the bishop, and round the shield something about his career. When completed the tapestries were hung above the choir stalls. The one we made at school was of Bishop Richard Fox, Bishop of Bath and Wells 1492-4, whose name we bore. His arms are a pelican pecking her breast to feed her young who are sitting below in a nest. This crest was also used by Corpus Christi College, Oxford, where father went. We wore the badge on our blazers. Round the shield were the rose of England and the thistle of Scotland, with the royal arms of the two countries. This commemorates the fact that in 1499-1500 Bishop Fox conducted the negotiations preceding the marriage of King James IV of Scotland with Princess Margaret, daughter of Henry VII. Their grandson James VI of Scotland became James I of England and united the two thrones.

In 2c we had extra art and music. One thing I have always valued was a series of lessons on handwriting. We were taught to write quickly and legibly, which has been invaluable. Towards the end of this year I began to work and shot ahead in maths to the great surprise of the maths mistress. Also in English literature and history which became much more interesting. As a result of good marks in the end of year examinations, Autumn 1942 saw me in the science third. Here we learned chemistry, physics and biology in addition to general subjects and I began to like school. We were able to stay in the lab after school some days a week to practice various experiments. My favourite subject was geography in which I later took a degree, and I spent a lot of time at home messing about with rocks and bits of the countryside. Also I liked chemistry sets. In those days children could buy sulphuric acid and hydrochloric acid over the counter at chemists in small blue bottles for a modest sum. Harry and I were always experimenting with these, having done all the experiments in the leaflets provided with the set. One day there was an explosion and acid flew all over the room, burning small holes all over the carpet, a constant reminder of our folly for years to come. Small holes were burnt in our clothes and our hands. From then on chemistry sets were banned from the house, but we quite happily continued in the museum and for years we continued to save for the giant set we were convinced would contain the recipe for gunpowder. Rumours used to go round the school children about the ingredients needed for making this desirable commodity, but we must always have used them in the wrong proportions. Holidays seemed longer then than now. All three terms were much the same length and we had four weeks off at Christmas and Easter, and eight weeks in the summer. To ensure this, Easter was not always in the Easter holidays! We always had Good Friday and Easter Monday off, but in 1940 when Easter fell on 24th. March, we went back to school afterwards until 11th. April when we broke up for the so-called Easter holidays. We worked on Whit Monday which was not a school holiday. Half-term fell on the middle Monday of the term, one day only. Needless to say it rarely if ever coincided with Harry's Monday. In September 1940 Harry became a boarder at King's, and stayed there altogether ten years until he left at eighteen. Three times a term we used to take him out on Saturday afternoon in his grey flannel suit and cap, always to the park. They were strained, stiff occasions which ended in tears all round and a gloomy journey home in the train. The spring term of 1941 I was a weekly boarder at a school friend's in Taunton, but hated it so much that it only lasted one term. Every Sunday I used to begin to cry after lunch which gradually wore everyone's resistance down.

In the summer of 1942 I became embarrassed by great wealth, a situation not encountered since. In wartime there was the difficult problem of school uniform and clothing coupons. Children of certain ages and those who were growing rapidly had extra coupons to cope with this. At eleven I was tall and we had the extra and we were able to buy the full uniform. Then in summer 1942 I had outgrown the original summer dresses and mother bought new ones. The school were anxious to have outgrown clothes in good condition to help parents cope with the difficulty of making coupons go round, and mother gave me four dresses to take to school. The domestic science mistress in charge of this asked how much they were. 'Nothing', I said. 'Nonsense, you must ask your mother how much she wants for them'. I took the message home. 'Don't be silly, of course we don't want anything for them', she said. I carried these messages to and fro, and then the domestic science mistress gave me £1 in half-crowns and said 'Ask your mother if this will be enough'. Mother was shocked - 'You must take the money straight back. Of course there will be children needing the clothes and they are welcome to them'. I timidly handed the money back, but it was not received. 'Of course you must have it, the clothes are hardly worn (surprise on my part), and people want to pay for their clothes (more surprise)'. So once more I took it home, but mother was adamant. 'Please don't be so silly, darling', she said. So I kept it. Eight half-crowns! I had never seen such a sum in actual hard cash before, and I didn't know what to do with it. It lay like a heavy weight on my conscience. Eventually I wrapped it up in an envelope and hid it in my writing case. We only had 3d. a week pocket money at that time, and it would have been impossible to spend such a large sum. It lay hidden for some years until eventually I discovered it when we had left Clayhanger, and then I had no difficulty in spending it. At Speech Day in July I quaked while mother was talking to the domestic science mistress whom I expected to say at any moment 'What did you do with the £1 I sent you Mrs. Drew?'

It was at another speech day that the Archdeacon of Taunton produced his mixed metaphor, very much appreciated by father in the audience, and the senior English mistress on the platform. He was addressing the Upper Sixth who were about to leave school. He said 'You are at the top of the tree with the ball at your feet. You must be careful that you do not grind your own axes'.

The war impinged a little at school. There was a branch of the League of Nations which I joined. It met after school and helped to fill in the long wait for the train agreeably. We were all very patriotic and used to sing the National Anthem at least twice a term at Assembly. The League of Nations met in the hall every fortnight or so, and we listened to talks on the Empire as it was still called, and our allies, and the virtues of peace and unity. Young people ardently believed these were possible then and we longed to help the war effort in order to achieve peace. But there was really little that children were able to do except to share in the austerity of food and clothing endured by the whole population. We were also affected by train delays, and most of us came from homes which had opened their doors to evacuees from towns.

There was a call at one stage of the war for sphagnum moss. This grew in the wastes of the Quantock Hills. Several days we had expeditions into the hills to gather it in baskets and boxes. Large quantities were collected and despatched. We never knew what it was used for, why it was used, or who used it. I've never heard of it before or since, but I could go to the place today where we dug it out, damp boggy land with tufts of cotton grass sprouting out. We combined our expedition with a visit to Nether Stowey where Coleridge and Wordsworth had lived for a time.

At the end of the war King George VI wrote an appreciation of their war effort to children, dated 8th. June 1946, and all school children were given a copy. It was headed by the Royal Coat of Arms and the date.

'Today, as we celebrate victory, I send this personal message to you and all other boys and girls at school. For you have shared in the hardships and dangers of a total war and you have shared no less in the triumph of the Allied Nations.

I know you will always feel proud to belong to a country which was capable of such supreme effort; proud, too, of parents and elder brothers and sisters who by their courage, endurance and enterprise brought victory. May these qualities be yours as you grow up and join in the common effort to establish among the nations of the world unity and peace'

George R. I.

Chapter 6.   BEACH COURT SCHOOL

Childish Recollections

> Oh! friend's regretted, scenes forever dear,   341
> Remembrance hails you with her warmest tear!
> Drooping, she bends o'er pensive Fancy's urn,
> To trace the hours which never can return.
>   Lord Byron

Soon after we arrived in Clayhanger in 1939, the billeting officer arrived to give us the good news that we had been allocated thirty evacuees, and that we should make suitable preparations to receive them as soon as possible. This was received with mixed feelings, our parents being filled with gloomy forebodings, Harry and I with pleasurable anticipation. Mother flatly refused to have even one evacuee without running water! Even if they were large enough to fetch their own bucket from the well! Almost immediately after this visit father received a letter from Miss Widlake, the headmistress of Beach Court Schoool, Walmer, Kent, where Harry and I had spent our first few years at school. She wrote asking him to look out for suitable accommodation for her school in the likely event of Walmer being declared a danger zone for children. This solved the problem in a satisfactory way, and gave us a breathing space before their arrival. The main rush of children had already left London, and been settled, and there was the lull of the 'phoney war. The placement officer was satisfied to allow us privately arranged evacuees to fill our large house, and we had some time to arrange for their arrival.

The most important thing to be done was to have a major water system installed in the house. This had been impossible to arrange for a private family in wartime, but if we were going to accommodate about thirty evacuees we should be allowed to install one. We were still carrying water from the well, washing up in the shallow brownstone sink and bathing in the galvanized iron bath. It was a nightmare to contemplate thirty-five people's consumption of water, all doubtless used to daily baths and water gushing out of taps. Father made enquiries amongst the local clergy, many of whom were similarly placed. He wrote to the Ecclesiastical Commissioners, familiar figures of my childhood, now become the Church Commissioners. They wrote back to the effect that it was no concern of theirs whether or when the clergy and their families bathed, but that we should try various charities set up to help clergy in situations of this sort. He wrote to a number of such charities, and Marshall's Charity, and Queen Anne's Bounty paid for our bath and water system. Queen Anne was our favourite monarch for years to come. It is to be doubted whether she had such luxurious bathrooms as those for which she posthumously paid for the clergy. As far as we were concerned, she was chiefly remembered for her forethought in bringing a little luxury into the spartan lives of clergy in remote country districts of England. It is sad that her small but useful charity, available to the clergy with a minimum of red tape, should be now just part of the large resources of the Church Commissioners, and no longer a separate charity. There is such a reassuring sound about a 'Bounty' which the word 'commissioners' does not possess, and I would be more confident in approaching the former rather than the latter in search of a bath.

We had to wait some time before the work could begin. A water diviner arrived first, fortunately while Harry and I were at home, and we walked with him all over the grounds whilst he searched for a convenient spring of water to tap, hazel twig in hand. He found the well to be the most reliable source, and of adequate capacity. Work began in mid-May 1940 and was still in progress a month later when the school arrived. It was very interesting for children to watch. Pipes were laid from the well to the house, quite a major undertaking as in places holes had to be bored through rock to take them. The well was at the bottom of a steep bank some hundred yards or so from the house, and considerably below. We watched the pipes gradually laid across the lawns and drive and reach the house. A pump was installed to pump up the water from the well, and large tanks were placed in the attics. Not only had the water to be pumped up from the well, it had to be pumped up to the third storey in order to provide enough pressure for the taps to work. Needless to say the pumping had to be done by hand as there was no electricity. A wooden pump handle was fitted up in the scullery, which was pushed backwards and forwards by one strong or two ordinary people. Eight hundred pumps filled the tank, and when the children had arrived a rota was made out covering all breaks, the dinner hour, before breakfast and the evening, to ensure a steady supply of water. The older the child, the more the pumps. It was hard work, but not too arduous in company, and songs were sung and gossip exchanged over the pump. Occasionally someone would forget to do their pumping and this would be discovered when no water came out of the taps, and there would be a rush to pump before the water remaining in the hot tank began to boil.

Most of the pipes had been laid by the time the school arrived, but the bathroom had not yet been installed. When France fell and our army returned to Britain, the south-east became a prohibited area, and the school had to leave within forty-eight hours. We received a telegram from Miss Widlake to say they were coming, and two days later we were meeting them in Taunton. The work was completed about a month later. A new sink was put into the kitchen. As it was in a very dark corner of the room, the only windows of which faced east over the courtyard, a window was cut in the west wall overlooking the enclosed garden. It was while cutting the window that a small round window was found in the middle of the thick walls probably Elizabethan.

Apart from the problem of putting in an adequate water system, there was also a great deal of furnishing to do. Mr. Parsons of the Boniface Home was a wonderful help and lent us enough iron bedsteads for the girls, which we put up in the Victorian part of the house and the attics. He also lent us some mattresses and blankets. Mother got vast amounts of china from the man who sold us paraffin, thick plain china plates and cups, soup bowls and enormous vegetable dishes, white quart jugs for milk and a vast meat plate. We spent a day in Tiverton buying pans and cutlery, carpets, bed linen and towels, blankets and curtains. As much as possible we got ready made, but mother spent hours running up curtains on her old-fashioned Jones sewing machine dated 1898, which is still in working order. Father bought the oil lamps and candlesticks and laid in a stock of candles. He bought bracket lamps for the dormitories and passages and attached them to the walls above the reach of small children. One of his main jobs which took considerable time each day, was cleaning and filling the lamps and trimming the wicks. He used to bring them down after breakfast and put them on a table in the butler's pantry. The kitchen and scullery had large old-fashioned hanging lamps of brass, attached to the ceiling by three chains which could be lowered and raised with a pulley. They each took about a quart of oil and gave out a good light. Our consumption of paraffin soared to fifty gallons a month in the winter. The main rooms downstairs had lamps with white fragile incandescent mantles. Each bedroom also had candles and matches in case a light was needed during the night. The lamps were turned off by a teacher at lights-out, and the biggest girl in the room had the candle and matches beside her bed. It must have seemed strange to the children to suddenly find themselves in the depths of the remote west country in a pre-electric era.

Great excitement reigned when the telegram arrived. I had reluctantly to go to school, but every other spare minute was spent in laying down carpets, putting up curtains and lamps, making up beds and filling hot 'pigs'. Thirty girls and small boys, three teachers, one mother and one very old godmother were to arrive on the London train in the early evening, which was the train for which the Barnstable line waited. So father came up to Taunton to help me meet them and conduct them home. The train steamed in and there they were pouring out of the carriages. What a lot of them, and all for us! We remembered most of those who were over eight, and Miss Widlake the headmistress. 'How you've grown' we all said to each other. What a mound of luggage, thirty odd trunks, crated boxes of books, handluggage, and coats. What a squash on the Barnstable train, not used to coping with such large unexpected numbers of passengers. The luggage quite filled the guard's van.

I forget how we all got to the Rectory that night, but the luggage came on the next day on the back of a lorry from the station. Mother was there to meet us at the door, and what a sorting out of rooms there was and a rushing about the garden of the younger children in the dark! Eventually everything was sorted out and we sat down to supper in a strangely different dining room. Our own small table was in the window, with long trestle tables from the hall with benches making an E to our table down the room, the mahogany sideboard against the west wall.

Looking after the school was my parents war work. For three and a half years father grew vegetables and kept hens to feed them, cleaned and trimmed the lamps, and taught them Latin and history. Mother cooked for them, three meals a day, on an old range and an oil cooker. In order to be able to do this in a large old house, they needed help. Winnie Tucker came several mornings a week and did all the personal washing, pillow cases and small towels. We used to carry great bundles of clothes up the hill to her house. It was very difficult to get a maid to live in during the war. Living-in maids virtually disappeared from the scene in 1939, and did not reappear again after the war as they had done in 1919. However, mother persevered, and in June 1940 a middle-aged deaf woman arrived from a home in Exeter. She was called Dora, and had been born deaf and dumb. She was not completely dumb, but her speech was almost unintelligible. Mother could understand her fortunately, but most people were too impatient to stand and listen. She was good at lip reading, and several of the children learned the deaf and dumb alphabet, and spoke to her with our hands. Dora had the lovely little room up a flight of stairs leading from the scullery, which we had used as a nursery. The dolls house came up to my room and the toys were dispersed. Dora was a very hard, but slow worker. She did mountains of washing up, all the scrubbing of the kichen and scullery and helped with the cleaning. But she was very temperamental and unco-operative. Once mother forgot her tea after supper, and at ten o'clock she found the washing-up had been left in the sink and a cryptic note on the table reading 'no tea, no washing-up'. She found life hard after the home and left in late 1941 after eighteen months. She went to a farmhouse in south Devon, but found life even harder there. In the late spring of 1942 we received a letter from her asking to come back. 'I am tired of skinning of the rabbits, and I am very fonding of the primroses (in Clayhanger)' she wrote. So she came back and mother gave her lighter work to do. We were in touch with the Deaf and Dumb Home in Exeter on her behalf, and once a year the church collections were sent to the home.

Apart from Dora and Winnie, we had a young girl straight from school. She was Joyce Palfrey from a small farm in Petton, and she came to us in the summer of 1940 aged fourteen, and stayed with us until we left. We all liked her. She cycled some three miles each way in all weathers five days a week, and sometimes Saturdays as well, from a remote farm on the hill. Her father and uncle played the accordian at the dances held in the tithe barn.

During the years they were with us there were always about thirty girls and small boys, ranging in age from five to eighteen. We knew most of the older ones, having been at school with them ourselves, and it was quite nostalgic to see the familiar green uniform and the different coloured exercise books with Beach Court School printed on the covers. Lessons were held in the tithe barn, which must have been more used during those years than ever before or since. Trestle tables were set up and the barn was so huge that two or three lessons could go on at a time. Lessons were also held in the dining room. Father's study became known as the little sitting room, and was used by the older girls as a common room. After tea the younger ones played in the dining room in winter before going to bed. In summer there was no difficulty about where to play with a big garden and outbuildings. Miss Widlake used our lounge and the staff must have gone to their own rooms. Apart from Miss Widlake, there was only one other permanent member of staff who was there all the time, Miss Ward, the deputy head. A number of others, mostly elderly, came and went, and usually had rooms in the village, just coming in to teach. One, a Miss Waggett, painted the house from the field below as Mrs. Mowat had done the previous year.

It was wonderful for Harry and I to have so many children living at home to play with. They were there most of the time, only those who had homes in safe places going home for the holidays. There was never a holiday with fewer than seven children left, and always Miss Widlake. There were a few small boys who quickly made friends with Harry, one, Hugh Bayly whom he had known at five. They were inseparable until Hugh went away to Blundells. He still used to come back for the holidays. He had two older sisters, Jane and Mary, who were with us all the time as their father was in Burma. In August 1940 their parents came and stayed to see the children, and their father then returned to Burma. He spent the entire time he was with us sitting on the lawn in a deckchair. 'Nothing would make me walk any distance', he used to declare, as he saw us setting off for all day picnics, equipped with knapsacks and strong shoes. After the Japanese invasion of Burma, he disappeared, and there were many anxious months for his children while they waited for news. He turned up footsore and weary in northern India, having walked over five hundred miles through hilly sub-tropical jungle! Later in the war, Mary became a Wren, and used to come home on leave making us very envious in her blue uniform. Her sister Jane had beautiful yellow ringlets. All of them had naturally curly hair, which Hugh hated. He used to smarm it down with water, but it always sprang up again. In the late autumn of 1942 Jane fell ill with a high temperature. She was very ill for several days, and Dr. Morgan came. He thought it might be infectious, and she was moved into my room, and I moved into the dormitory, which was fun for me. There was a lot of talking and giggling and muffled snorts of laughter after lights out. Then Jane's temperature dropped, and after a few days she got up. But she was strangely lethargic, and mother was worried about her. However, the doctor said she was now fit, and just weak after the temperature she returned to school. A day or two later she felt very weak and asked mother if she could rest. It was a Saturday, and all afternoon I sat with her in her room, and read to her as she couldn't hold the book. She was the same on Sunday, and on Monday she was paralysed, and the doctor rushed out to confirm what was then known as infantile paralysis. As the highly infectious stage of the disease was over, she stayed at home and mother nursed her for nearly a month. She was very weak and helpless, but gradually with rest and care regained some use of her limbs. Then in December there was a place for her at Exeter Orthopaedic Hospital, where she stayed for several months. We visited her there sometimes, when we were able, and all the girls used to write and send her little gifts. She came home in the spring, and made a very good recovery, only limping a little. A few months later she was eighteen and left school, and was actually able to become a landgirl.

As soon as infantile paralysis was confirmed, we were all put in strict quarantine for three weeks. This was wonderful for me as I didn't have to go to school, but joined in at Beach Court. It was lovely to be at home all day, and I enjoyed the small classes. Fortunately no one else developed the disease.

Another family of three were the Collins. Elizabeth was about seven when the school arrived, and she had twin brother and sister aged three. They stayed during the summer holidays with their mother, and later, when they were five, came to school. My oldest friend, Mary Peerless, with whom I had started school at five, came with her widowed mother and very old godmother, 'Goddy'. Mary and her mother lived in the farm at the top of the hill going towards Venn Cross. Goddy lived in the opposite direction, across the glebe meadow, in a lonely farm on the Ashbrittle road. Mary and I used to walk over to see her sometimes, and always had tea. Mary used to come rushing down the hill in the early morning, usually late for school. In the summer holidays of 1940 we spent a lot of time up at the farm, helping. We worked so hard there that summer we really thought we were indispensible, but looking back, I'm sure the farmer breathed a sigh of relief when term started. We had a craze for milking. and every afternoon would see us up in the milking shed, sitting on three-legged wooden stools, resting our heads on the soft warm flanks of a cow as we struggled to produce milk. The cowman and the farmer's wife got a steady flow of milk into their buckets, and would be soon carrying them foaming into the yard, but we could hardly ever produce more than a few reluctant drops. But it was fun, and there was a warm milky smell in the shed. Sometimes we were given a glass of warm milk. The farmer and his wife were a middle-aged childless couple and were very kind to us. We liked them as they didn't look down on children, but treated us naturally as fellow-workers, and spoke to us as equals.

We were better at haymaking, and most of August saw us in the hayfields, all day in the sun, with our lunch in a basket by the hedge. The hay was cut by machine, but had to be lifted by hand into the cart. It was lifted by pitchfork, and the labourers used to lift great loads and toss them on to the cart. That was also an art, and all we could manage were a few wisps, which kept falling off the fork as we vainly tried to throw it on to the cart. The first few days we were bright red, but by the end of the summer we were dark brown. We worked up a terrific appetite, and ate enormous sandwiches, sitting against the hedge with the other workers. It was this summer we began to drink cider, and it was a pretty rough brew. Most of the farms were surrounded by cider apple orchards, and in one of the large sheds there would be a cider press. Some were over one hundred years old. The cider produced was dark and strong. It was kept in casks, and glasses were handed to visitors. We used to buy a cask of local cider from which we helped ourselves. Fortunately we still found it too strong to drink more than a very small glass at a time.

There was another girl my age we were fond of, Margaret McNaughton, who was there with her older sister. We used to go for walks together over the fields. She was staying with her parents at a nearby village during the holidays later in the war, and was tragically killed when her bicycle ran into a lorry. The older girls went to her funeral taking flowers from the garden.

Parents in the late twenties and thirties thought up some unusual names for their children, as indeed they always do. We had a Marsali and a Jellis (pronounced Yellis), a Pansy and a Cherry. an old-fashioned Pippa. During the war, father was asked to baptize a child Sireen (after the sirens), but insisted on a Christian name as well. During the first World War, he remembered someone naming their child Dardanella Jane. The butcher in Deal had been Inkerman Baker. Pippa was a painter, and painted a lovely view of the top of the drive seen from the house, the avenue of trees, and part of the croquet lawn. Marsali was keen on planes, and drew them endlessly. She always carried a book of silhouettes of planes (as seen from ground level looking up) so as to be able to recognize any that flew over. I have a picture of hers, a 'Buffalo' in my autograph book. Harry from Taunton obtained the signature of the youngest son of the Emperor Haile Selassie who was in his class at school. His elder sister was nursing in Bath during the war, where her family were living in exile since the fall of their country to the Italians.

We had one sad and unattractive little girl called Ruth. Her parents took the war as an opportunity to get rid of their child for long periods of time. She was with us almost all the time, and one year even at Christmas. She received plenty of presents but no letters during the term, and hardly ever a visit from her mother. She was younger than us and used to trail round after us during the holidays, miserably. We didn't realize her predicament and used to say 'O go away, Ruth'. Once she did go away for a few days. On her return she looked at us all for a long time, then said, 'Same old Rectory, same old rector, same old school, and same old cat', and burst into tears. We realized then that life wasn't for everyone the paradise it was for us in the holidays.

With so many children growing up together it was like living in a tribe. We had customs and taboos and games which grew up over the years.

Whenever we went to or from the station in any numbers we used to divide into two teams, and the first lot would set off a few minutes before the rest. The object was to get to the station without being seen by ones opponents. If you saw anyone, you shouted 'dead', and that person was then out of the game and could walk safely along the road. The rest would continue along the top of the banks, inside the fields, or wildly dashing across the road, when one came to an impossible bank, heart in mouth. Sometimes there would be an ambush at a likely place, perhaps the clump of trees at the top of Well Hayes Hill, and the whole of the following team might be out at once. But sometimes we would all reach the station unobserved, the first lot warmly esconced in the waiting room, crouching down below the level of the windows to the bewilderment of the other occupants, and the following ones hiding behind the hedge of the field across the road from the station ready to resume the game on the homeward walk.

The first few months, and always in the summer, we played 'lands'. This was only ever played in the field across the road from the upper drive. The bank was high and there were rough steps cut up the bank to a wooden stile which led into the field. The field was really two fields, both fairly small, separated by a very old bank which had broken away in several places. Both fields were rough pasture, sometimes occupied by cows. A high bank separated them from the road and there were high thick hedges all round. As they were on the slope of a hill, as ninety per cent of the fields of north Devon are, there was quite a difference in height between the top of the right hand field, and the bottom of the left hand field as viewed from the stile. The lower field ran down to the stream which, across the road, flowed along the foot of our garden. The bank which separated them had a few old trees along it. There was a small rise on the right but a steep sharp drop down to the lower field. In this field there was the ruin of an old cottage, roofless and derelict, perhaps empty for twenty years. We divided into two teams and drew lots for which field to have as ones base. We always drew lots as none of us ever had a coin to toss. The oldest would hold two sticks and a member of the opposite team would pull one out, and if it were the longest, choose her field. Invariably the winner chose the top field, which had most of the advantages. The game was very simple, a form of 'touch'. The object was to touch a member of the opposite team on your home ground, when she would become a prisoner and have to go with you to the jail, usually an inaccessible corner of the field. Members of her team would then try to release her (by touch), without themselves being caught. One was safe both on ones home ground and on the bank between, which was no-man's-land. But no-man's-land was very difficult to balance on unless one rushed up and grabbed a branch to hold on to. Coming from above one could swing down on a branch and land quite far out in the lower field. We used to play for hours in the long hot summer days and until it became too wet in winter. Then both fields were so muddy and the bank too slippery to play properly. Our clothes used to get into a frightful state with both the stalking game to the station and lands.

Another game we played frequently was soldiers. We were permanently divided into two regiments, British and German, and as the war progressed we rose in rank. We would decide by lot at the beginning which side was to be German, the least popular needless to say. The ranks of course were British as none of us knew the German ranks or ever suspected them of being any different. I began the war as a private, and rose to be a second lieutenant. When we left I was fifteen, and there were still girls three years older who had all the higher ranks. Looking back it seems strange that we all played, from five year olds to the eighteens, although the older ones used to have armchair or deck chair commands, and conduct campaigns from behind their books in the garden. It was the middle ranks who were the most keen, the eights to twelves, and we played endlessly. We all carried swords, as it was not a modern war we were fighting, but something out of the age of chivalry. Our swords were sharpened stair rods with a short cross-piece nailed across. We used to drill for a bit and then fight, actually with swords, or more usually a game similar to our ambushes. We played right through the war and it never palled.

In the winter when the nights drew in there were different activities. During the week most of us were busy in the evenings with homework, and I was late from school. But there were weekends and holidays. Reading aloud was popular. One of the older girls would read while the rest of us knitted. Even the little girls knitted. There was an endless amount of knitting to be done in wartime. One winter the older girls were knitting kharki helmets and the rest of us endless kharki scarves, endless in length and endless in numbers to small fingers. One year we were lucky and were knitting for the navy in navy blue. But the wool was very coarse, thick oiled wool, trying to the fingers. But how proud we were to do it and to know that we were making something of real use.

One winter, 1942-3 we had first aid classes from a St. John's instructor. We all had a copy of the St. John's manual and worked through it, practising on each other. The most popular were the fractures. In the class we used proper three-cornered slings, but we all soon had our own, cut out of old sheets, which we kept for weeks in our pockets to practise with at odd moments. The older ones went in for a test at the end of the course and received certificates. The classes were held in our house as there was no small village hall, only the large tithe barn. Several women from the village came up to the classes which we all enjoyed.

Most of the winter activities took place in the little sitting room. Often father would come in and play the piano for singing from the Scottish Student Song Book or nursery rhymes. It was an old-fashioned upright piano dated 1887, with brass candle-holders. During the years in Clayhanger they were filled with candles and we clustered round the paino to peer over his shoulder at the flickering light on the music and words. At the end of the winter term of 1940 on 16th. December, the girls gave a concert and acted the Christmas Carol by Charles Dickens, to an audience of the smaller children, the Drew's (us), and the domestic staff. That was the start of a tradition in our family to read the Christmas Carol every Christmas. Father began two evenings before Christmas, and by Christmas night would finish the story. Every Christmas until after we were grown up and gone, even the sad Christmas when Harry was fighting in Korea and we had no recent news of him, and until the year I went to the Middle East, we continued; and that was the last Christmas we spent together as a family.

The winter of 1940-41 was hard and cold for Devon. Snow fell on the night of 31st. December, and the New Year dawned white and sunny. All day we built a huge snowman on the lawn and had fights on and off. A few days later in the field we built huge walls of snow and fought behind them, bombarding each other with snowballs. Later in January 1941 there was a freezing fog and we woke one morning to a fairy world. Every smallest twig and blade of grass was encased in a sheath of ice. It was bright and sunny and every puff of wind tinkled through the trees. It was freezing cold and our breath steamed as we ran about and played. When term began it was not such fun leaving the nice warm house at 7.30 in the morning in the freezing dark. We had no fur-lined boots then, but I used to wear a pair of woolly socks on top of my black stockings, inside my wellingtons. It was cold again in the evening coming home, but wonderful winter weather at weekends compared to the usual Devon rain and mud.

In January we used to go to the pantomime in Exeter by train, changing at Morebath Junction Halt, and trundling slowly down the lovely Exe valley. In 1940 we went with Nurse Fagg an old friend of our childhood, who visited us every year until her death in the late fifties. She was gloomy about the weather and grumbled about leaving a nice warm house to 'hare off all over the country'. Her forebodings were justified. Snow was falling as we came out of the theatre. The train was delayed, and we had a freezing wait at Morebath for the Barnstable-Taunton train. On arrival at Venn Cross there were already deep drifts, and we battled home through blinding snow in the dark, arriving late at night. Great fun for Harry and me.

In the morning we had been to the cathedral and explored the lovely old city of Exeter, spending most of our time in the Tudor street of old bookshops. Later in the war Exeter was badly bombed and that street wiped out of existence, so that when we went again it was quite different, covered with derelict rubble.

On 8th. January 1943 we went to Exeter to see Jane in hospital. To our surprise she was in bed outside on a verandah, with bright red cheeks and frozen hands. After seeing her we went on to the pantomime. This was the most wonderful pantomime of our childhood. There were two scenes we always remembered. An old-fashioned stage coach trundled on to the back of the stage, and the driver got down and opened the door for two passengers who were waiting. 'Well, we'd better get in', and they clambered in with so much luggage that the coach sank into the mud. 'Well, we'd better get out', and out they emerged on the other side. Eventually they went off leaving all their luggage behind. The other scene was of a poor old night-watchman on a cold night, shivering beside a stove. He kept getting closer and eventually sat down on top of the nice warm stove. Big smiles. Then he began to wriggle a bit, and look bewildered. Then with a terrible scream he leapt into the air, and turned round clapping his hands to his bare burnt bottom. This was such a popular item it was repeated by the other clown. Harry and Hugh rolled about all over the place in their mirth. That year we had hired a coach as Jane's hospital was some way outside the city, and we were able to take all the girls to see her and then go on to the pantomime. It was luxurious to return in the winter dark by coach and not to face the cold walk from the station.

In the spring when many of the children had gone home for the Easter holidays and the numbers were down to a dozen or so, mother would spring clean. Those who were left would eagerly help. On a fine windy day all the mattresses were carried out to air in the courtyard, draped over walls and chairs, and some eighty or ninety blankets would be washed by hand and hung out to dry in endless lines. One day we went off for a picnic. After lunch it clouded over and heavy rain began to fall. We rushed home and staggered in with the soggy bundles and draped them all over the little sitting room, and built a huge fire. For several days it resembled a Turkish bath, and the whole house seemed warm and damp. However, when they were dry it made a wonderful place to play when no one was looking.

Feeding so many people in wartime was quite a problem. The basic rations arrived, but making them go round was a constant headache. The butter problem was solved by giving everyone their own labelled dish of butter, usually two ounces. I used to divide mine into eight, one piece for each day and two for Sunday. In practice I ate it all at breakfast as I was never home for tea, and often had fried bread or bread and dripping for supper. Everyone also had either one pound of jam or marmalade. What a problem! To eat marmalade every day for tea, or jam for breakfast! There was less problem over the meat. Throughout the war we kept forty odd hens, and the older ones were regularly killed and boiled for chicken broth, and then the carcase popped into the oven in hot fat to crisp up. One year there was foot and mouth disease locally and all the well animals were killed as well as the sick. We were all able to have as much lamb as we could eat. Unfortunately it was before the days of domestic freezers, and all meat was eaten fresh. Sometimes it was possible to get rabbit which was not rationed.

Father grew a large number of vegetables, potatoes, cabbages, leeks and onions, cauliflowers and beet. One year we hopefully grew sweet corn. But it didn't ripen, and it was years before we tried again. One year we had masses of marrows, and anyone who wanted could choose a marrow. We carved our names lightly in the skin, and had a race for the biggest. It was won easily by Timmy, the blue Persian, whose marrow reached gigantic proportions, and was carried proudly to church for the harvest festival. We grew sunflowers for the hens. Poor hens. They were allowed a very small ration of corn. Mother used to boil up a bucket of potato peelings and vegetables and odd pieces of bread, and it was tipped into a little trough while they all gathered hopefully round, treading on our feet and squawking rudely. We used to like to collect eggs from the nice warm strawfilled nests.

In the autumn mother would preserve as many eggs as she could in 'waterglass'. This was a smelly powder mixed with water in a large crock. The eggs were lowered into the liquid which preserved them. Sometimes she managed as many as two or three hundred, and in January and February when the hens were laying badly we would use the waterglass eggs to fry or poach. There was also, of course, the ration of dried eggs used in scrambled eggs, and for puddings and cakes.

Winnie's sister's husband kept bees, and every autumn we were able to buy twenty-four pounds of clover honey from him. It was a very dark honey with a delicious wild flavour. Also in the autumn one could get an extra ration of sugar for jam. Every year we went to a field full of bramble bushes, and picked most of the day, taking home huge quantities of blackberries. In 1940 the blackberries ripened early, and on 5th. August we picked seven pounds in an afternoon. later in the month we picked twenty pounds in one day. Mother made huge blackberry and apple pies, and turned the rest into jelly. After boiling up in the evening, the blackberries were tipped into a large old muslin jelly bag, and dripped all night into an earthenware bowl. Next morning the liquid and sugar were boiled again until the jelly would set. Everyone would gather round to help her, as in those days tops for the jam jars had to be cut out by hand. Circles were drawn on greaseproof paper to put straight on the jelly, then larger circles for the tops. As the war progressed, rubber bands disappeared, and the circles had to be tied on with cotton. Then the jars were labelled. Mother made marrow and ginger jam, and we would all help cutting up the marrow into little cubes, and in the late spring rhubarb jam was made. In January 1940 she made marmalade as usual, but that was the last spring the Seville oranges were availabe, and after the marmalade was used up we had to depend on bought supplies.

Women's Institutes in wartime made jam for sale on the ration. If the jam was below a certain standard they were able to see it locally, off the ration. One year a nearby branch of the W.I. had sub-standard jam to sell, and mother bought one hundred pounds of blackberry and apple. The Institute gave us the eight pounds they had left over to finish it off, and were pleased to sell such a large amount for their funds. The jam had huge lumps of apple in it and the appearance was poor, which was why it hadn't been passed by the Ministry of Food. But it was useful for pies and a steam pudding mother made which we called 'stodge', a very filling and fattening pudding eaten with custard. We also got delicious apple chutney from the same W.I. which was not on the ration.

In the autumn Mr. Parsons sold us twelve pounds of tomatoes at a time, which were delicious, grown under glass by the boys of the home, and later tomatoes grown outside in his fine sheltered garden.

When the school first came we still had cream. We fetched it from a farm across the fields in the direction of Petton. We had been getting it since our arrival once a week, and Harry and I used to walk over the fields in the early days with Mrs. Hukstable, the post-woman. The farmer's wife had a lovely cool dairy with great bowls of cream. We watched her making the Devonshire clotted cream, heating it slowly and gradually skimming off the cream. We bought it in a small churn, and used to eat it for tea with strawberry jam on big floury buns. In June 1940 and for two or three more months the girls used to fetch the cream in a bigger churn, and buns with jam and cream were the favourite tea of the week. Then in late 1940 no more could be made, all extra milk had to be turned into butter.

We had all our meals in the dining room, and a brass bell was knocked by a spoon to summon everyone. All our large silver serving spoons were used although there was a wooden knocker. But it was never there, and one of the permanent legacies of the war are our battered spoons. Grace was said by the older girls in turn, and at Sunday lunch grace was sung. The sung grace was taken from Psalm 145, verses 15 and 16. 'The eyes of all wait upon Thee, O Lord: and Thou givest them their meat in due season. Thou openest thine hand: and fillest all things living with plenteousness'.

In late 1943 father was offered a living in Berkshire by his old college, Corpus Christi, Oxford. He and mother were getting very tired, and the school was dwindling in numbers, and he decided to accept. In 1941 Miss Widlake had made him a very fine tooled leather writing case with his entwined initials on the front and BC (Beach Court) 1941 on the back. As a farewell gift the girls embroidered a tablecloth. In the centre was Beach Court School 1940-43. The names of the four staff were in each corner in cream silks, and Miss M. L. Widlake in cream beside the name of the school. All round the cloth were embroidered the names of all the boys and girls who had been with us. The children who were still there embroidered their own names in the colour of their choice, and the older girls embroidered the rest. Families were in groups, in the same colour. Even Dusty and Rex their pets appear. It is a lovely cloth and was the treasured possession of mother's until her death - a memory of four years hard work.

Chapter 7.   THE VILLAGE AND PEOPLE

A Devonshire Song

They say that love's more fickle of wing
Than it was in the days gone by;
But a Devonshire lane dives deep in the spring,
Ere it lifts through the fern to the sky.
As it was in the days of good Queen Bess,
When the sweet of the year's in the cider-press,
And the whistling maid turns home.

For the south wind comes, and it brings wet weather,
And the west is cloaked with grey,
And a whistling maid and a crowing hen
Are wicked as frost in May;
But snow - white snow, - in a Devonshire night,
Is only the bloom on the spray,
And a good cob wall, and a good hat and shoes,
And a good heart will last for aye.
                                        Alfred Noyes

Clayhanger is a tiny hamlet five hundred feet up in the extreme northeast of Devon, being about a mile from the Somerset border in the east, and about two miles from the same border in the north, just beyond Venn Cross. The next villages east and north are in Somerset. It lies on a hill between two valleys and is actually on the watershed between the Exe and the Tone, a geographical fact which loomed large and important in my mind as I learnt of the existence of watersheds. The tiny stream which flowed along the foot of our garden between the Rectory and the village had risen perhaps a mile away and flowed westwards to join the Batherm at Nutcombe, which in turn flowed into the Exe south of Stawley in Somerset. The road between Clayhanger and the upper cross roads, about one mile long ran along the watershed between the two. Going up from the village at Bonny Cross was the tiny red brick telephone exchange, the Clayhanger exchange, in a small enclosure. Beyond the cross on the left one could see a muddy patch where the nameless stream which flowed east rose. Although the village was so small, about 350 people all told, it had two important features in my mind. It had its own telephone exchange, and it was on a major watershed between two mighty rivers, the Exe and the Tone, at least the mightiest rivers that I was acquainted with! One afternoon Harry and I spent a happy and muddy time closely examining the source of this stream whilst I explained its importance to him, while a look of complete incomprehension settled on his face. I'm sure the georgraphy mistress would have been gratified if she had known.

Looking south from our house one looked across the valley to Clayhanger about the same height as us, two farms, the church and a row of cottages on top of a hill. Beyond, the land rose again to Bonny Cross, and beyond again to 750 feet. Near the top of the farthest hill was the last farm in the parish, Crosses Farm. The village itself was tiny and there were many scattered farms and cottages. The church dominated the view with its high north Devon tower. Outside the porch was a mounting block for the rector and others to mount their horses. Although it was only half a mile away, it was downhill then steeply uphill along a winding road. One passed the two farms and then the church and cottages. At the end of the row of cottages a cul de sac ran back to the church and the front doors and gardens of the cottages faced onto this road. At the end was the gate leading into the large churchyard. Continuing along the road there was a farm road leading to Nutcombe Manor only, which was gated and had grids across it at the field boundaries. The road then passed a group of cottages with bright gardens on the right, the tiny post office on the left, the old school and then two council houses on the right. The road then ran between steep banks uphill to Bonny Cross and beyond to Crosses Farm.

Turning east at Bonny Cross, the road was known as Featherbed Lane, and ran past a modern bungalow and then South Hele farm before turning north and running down to Venn Cross. Turning west at Bonny Cross the road was very narrow and ran between high banks, a real Devon lane. On the right were several small woods known as copses, the largest being Nutcombe Copse which to us was a forest. We often played there, and it is a light open wood with many oaks. Beyond the copse was the watersplash, where a wooden footbridge spanned the stream. We used to linger here for some time, and the two and a half miles to Petton by road could take a considerable time with all the possible delightful diversions along it. Beyond the watersplash was another copse on the left, with North Bulcombe farm on the track below. On the road was a wooden ledge for milk churns, as there was outside every dairy farm. A steep rise led to Petton, a few farms and the chapel of ease some 530 feet up. Just beyond the church the 'serviceable' road joined the main Taunton-Barnstable road which ran along the railway a good part of the way.

When we first went to Clayhanger in 1939 the farms were almost entirely under pasture. The fields were small with high banks and hedges, and very steep, especially on the sides of the valleys. The soil was red and infertile, derived from the Old Red Sandstone. The fields were filled with dairy cattle and sheep, and the chief product was milk and cream, rich creamy milk from Jersey and Guernsey cows and Red Devons. Round the farms were cider apple orchards. As the war progressed farmers came under pressure to plough up their land to produce food which under normal conditions was imported. For the first time in history these small steeply sloping fields were ploughed up and sown with corn and kale, sugar beet and potatoes. Some of the ploughing was done by horses as the fields were too steep for tractors. In the autumn and winter children were allowed off school for the potato picking and kale cutting. After the war the fields reverted once more to their natural pasture.

The sheep were taken to market in Bampton, and apart from the weekly small local market, there were two main markets for sheep and cattle in the late spring and October. Once a year there was also the pony market, in October, when the rough Exmoor ponies were rounded up on the moors and brought down to be sold for pit ponies. How wild and free they looked with their manes tossing and their rough short coats. We were sad for them doomed to spend their lives in the dark below the ground, far from the freedom they had known on the moors.

The farms were gaunt and life was harder then than now. There was no electricity in the village and water was drawn from wells. The living room kitchen opening into the yard was stone-flagged with a huge open fireplace where a large log would be smouldering, the only source of heat. There would perhaps be a pump over the shallow sink, or else in the yard outside. Many farms had dairies, cool, with slate shelves where bowls of cream stood, and churns for butter-making on the floor. The children who lived in the farms had to help, and boys and girls milked before going to school in the mornings. I knew a girl of ten who was responsible for milking four cows morning and evening. The old wooden pattens were still in use. These were slipped on over shoes to go out into the muddy yards. Many still made their own or got them from the carpenter. The patten had a high sole so that ones feet kept out of the mud, a forerunner of wellingtons and much cheaper.

There were roughly the same number of people in the village as there had been in 1850 when William White wrote his gazetteer of Devon. In 1850 there had been 294, which included a tailor, two shopkeepers, two shoemakers, ten farmers, one publican (of a beer house), and a rector. In 1940 there was no tailor or shopkeeper, no shoemaker or publican. The beer house had gone. There was one very small sub-post office in the dark front room of a cottage, served by Mr. Pringle, 'poor old Pringle' as he was known. We bought our stamps there and things like string. One day life became too much for him, and he was found hanging in the morning from his stairs. The person who found him came running for father, who was very reluctant to go. However, he did go, after calling the doctor by phone. Later he buried him in the churchyard with very few mourners, and thought that was the end of him. But no. Someone, whom we never discovered, wrote to the bishop to ask if permission had been given to bury a suicide in consecrated ground. In former times they had been buried at Bonny Cross. The bishop was unmoved, and the poor old man's bones left in peace. That was the last of the post office. No one was appointed to take his place, and no one wanted to live in the cottage.

Mrs. Huxstable was the postwoman. She went round on foot dressed in a long warm gaberdene and scarf and thick wellington boots. In the early days we used to accompany her on her very considerable round. When we saw her coming up the drive we used to rush for our wellingtons to be ready to go. From the rectory she crossed the road, climbed the stile and walked across the fields to Nutcombe Manor. There were almost always letters for us and the manor. Then on to the outlying farms. She was always cheerful, and I only once heard her grumble when she had a postcard with 1d. stamp on it to deliver to a farm over a mile away on a cold bleak January day in a steady drenching downpour. But she went, and we went with her, quite cheerfully. She was ageless, tireless and cheerful, and we talked about mutual interests, the state of the fields and crops, the early lambs which were just arriving, and the weather and conditions under foot.

In 1939 and 1940 letters were still 1½d. and postcards and Christmas cards in unsealed envelopes were 1d. By 1943 they had risen to 2½d. and 2d. respectively, printed papers being 1d. These rates remained unchanged for some time to come. The charges to the British Empire were the same as inland, 1½d. in 1939 and 2½d. in 1943. Also the postal system was efficient. A letter posted one afternoon in London, would be delivered the following morning to the remotest farm in north Devon, having travelled by rail, van and in a bag on foot for the last few miles. Railway fares were also low, and the railway was a great boon during the war when it was almost the only form of transport in north Devon, quick, reliable, warm and cheap. The fares were 1½d. per mile and three farthings for a cheap day return. An adult's season ticket was 1d. per mile and a child's three farthings. My season ticket to Taunton was between £5 and £6 per term and the journey twenty miles each way.

It was a red letter day when a letter arrived for me, and I still have three received during the war in Clayhanger, found in an old box after my return from years in the Middle East. One is a postcard from mother who had gone for a few days to stay in Malvern. She wrote that it was a pleasant town, but the countryside 'is not lovely like our own Devonshire', and to say that she had bought me a green china rabbit. The second letter was from Canon B. K. Cunningham, Principal of Westcott House, Cambridge, and Chaplain to King George VI. He had baptized Harry and me in the college chapel in 1937 when father was an ordinand there. I had written to tell him of my confirmation in March 1943. He was a bachelor, and almost totally deaf, very good with children, and we remembered him with warm feelings of affection. In Cambridge 1937 the ordinands had mostly been young, and father in his thirties with two young children, the oldest. 'B.K.' as he was known, was in late middle age. I remember the water trickling down my nose after I had been baptized. After the service he asked us to tea in his rooms, and we had a wonderful tea of cake and chocolate biscuits, but no butter on the bread. He had forgotten the butter. Afterwards we played 'sardines' and he and Harry and I hid in a tiny brush cupboard, but gave ourselves away when he let out an enormous dusty sneeze.

The third was a postcard, also from someone we had met in Cambridge, the Revd. Austin Williams, whom we knew as Sam. It came from Germany, where he had been interned a prisoner of war, and was written on a P.O.W. card, a few lines long, which he had written in tiny writing. We wrote regularly to him during the war, but naturally the few letters he was allowed to write were mainly to his family. He was Harry's godfather. We were very excited about this card. He wrote about the birds and countryside round about where he was interned. Another friend from Cambridge, Tulliedeigh Ogilvy, had joined the Tank Regiment as a Chaplain in 1940. He came to see us late in 1939 on a very wet day, and we played games of snakes and ladders and cards. Abracadabra he shouted when he won! He was later killed in the fighting in north Africa.

In 1850 one of the shoemakers had been a Vicary. In 1939 there was a still a Vicary in the village, the carpenter. He lived in the end cottage of the row leading to the church. He was a real craftsman, surrounded by wood and tools. Shortly after our arrival he came up the drive wheeling a beautiful large wooden wheelbarrow to show father, and offered it to him for thirty-five shillings. He had made it to order for a farmer who considered that to be an exhorbitant price. Father had it for years and it was the best wheelbarrow he ever had. One day he was wheeled home in it. He had been down at the bottom of the drive tidying up the undergrowth with a billhook, when he was afflicted by a sudden attack of lumbago, and lay unable to move on the grass. Fortunately some of the older girls came along and wheeled him home.

Poaching was still prevelent in the country during the war years. In a book from the library 'A History of the Forest of Exmoor' by Edward T. MacDermott, we were delighted to come across a former Clayhanger poacher. In 1260 the foresters presented to Philip of Luccumbe and Richard of Bradeleghe, the verderers of the Forest of Exemore, one Viger, the son of Fulk of Cleyhangre, a henchman of Richard Beaumund. Richard, his huntsman, Viger and Beyvin, a tailor had taken many stags and hinds from the forest without warrant. These poachers lived outside the forest, and the foresters had not been able to detain them. So the Sheriff of the county where they lived, Devon, was ordered 'to cause them to come' to the county court. In this particular case they were ordered to come to Wiltune (Wilton, near Salisbury) on the Sunday next before the Nativity of St. John the Baptist, when the court would next meet, 22nd. June 1270. After five offences a culprit was outlawed. The clergy in those days were themselves not above a spot of poaching. In 1270 Walter, son of Mathew parson of Ar (Oare), and John, his father's servant, found a dead hind in the forest and took it home. Here father 'knowingly harboured them with the same venison'. The two villeins were imprisoned and the parson fined twenty shillings, a considerable sum in those days.

The farmers in Clayhanger were mainly local except for the farmer at the entrance to the village, who was a Londoner. He had come in the 1920's and settled here because of his health, and had founded a large dairy herd. There was a dear old lady living in one of the farms when we arrived, a Mrs. Blew. She had delightful old-fashioned manners, and curtsied to the rector whenever she met him. She was hale and hearty, and once, meeting him outside the top gate, challenged him to a race, and they both hared off down the hill. She spoke in a broad dialect, and used a number of words no longer current. Talking about the twilight she said 'in the dimsey'. Like everyone else she referred to everyone and everything regardless of gender as 'him' or ''e'. It was confusing at first when she said 'is 'e in?' meaning mother and not father.

Clayhanger and all the isolated higher villages were very healthy places. In Tudor time it was one of the few places in 1541 to escape 'the bloody flux', a virulent type of dysentry rampant in the west a year after a severe drought, when many wells had dried up. Ten years later it escaped entirely 'the great sweat', a kind of 'flu. It was still a healthy place. Apart from one case of infantile paralysis, everyone was fit and well apart from childish ailments. Once after playing too much in the fields, a number of the girls developed 'cowpox', a rash on their hands, highly contagious, but quickly cured.

Another more serious effect of isolation was the lack of jobs for school leavers. They had no choice of occupation. None went to the grammar school while we were there, and all left Shillingford School at fourteen, the boys to be farm labourers and the girls to help at home or go into domestic service. In wartime that meant until they were old enough to become landgirls or join the services. But work on farms was interesting, and one could specialize in those days. Some labourers were chiefly hedgers and ditchers, and made a beautiful job of the banks and hedges, lavishing loving care on their appearance. Others would be cowmen, shepherds or general workers. They were the last of the non-mechanical farm workers in our land, even the tiny, steep fields of Devon, becoming mechanized after the war.

Chapter 8.   THE PARISH

A Devonshire Ditty

> When we die - we'll think of Devon
> Where the garden's all aglow
> With the flowers that stray across the gray old walls:
> Then we'll climb it out of heaven,
> From the other side you know,
> Struggle over it from heaven
> With the apple blossom snow,
> Tumble back again to Devon
> Laugh and love as long ago,
> Where there isn't any fiery sword at all.
>
>   Alfred Noyes.

The parish of Clayhanger with Petton when father was rector, covered a over nine thousand acres. In 1850 at the time when William White produced his gazateer of Devon, Clayhanger was a parish on its own, and Petton was a chapel of ease under the Rector of Bampton.

The parish included the hamlets of Clayhanger and Petton, each with a church, and the hamlets of Venn Cross and Shillingford without churches. There had been a church at Shillingford which was falling into ruin in 1850. The Victorians did not rebuild it. Ironically Shillingford then grew, and in 1940 had the largest population, the only school and the only inn. The chapel was by then a complete ruin. In 1850 the population had been 325 in Clayhanger, 322 in Petton and 322 in Shillingford. In 1940 there were still about 900 people, rather more in Shillingford, and fewer in Petton.

The parish lay in the extreme north-east of the Exeter Diocese, being about twenty-five miles from the cathedral. It was in the Tiverton Archdeaconry and the Cullompton Deanery. There were far more clergy then than now in this remote part of Devon, most villages and hamlets with a church still having their own resident priest. Father devoted his time impartially to the whole area, visiting each farm and cottage on foot in all weathers, accompanied by Nipper his retriever who carried his stick. One day a week he devoted to Shillingford, a walk of over four miles each way, before he began work. There he called on the children in the school before going on into the village. Shillingford as its name implies was lower than Clayhanger, 'Clayhanger' meaning a wooded hill of clay, the clay in this case being the heavy reddish mud derived from the Old Red Sandstone. Shillingford, about 410 feet up was built around an ancient ford across the river Batherm, here grown quite wide and impressive, although still shallow. The school was east of the village, a gaunt Victorian building. There was a small delightful inn, 'The Barleycorn'. The ruined chapel was off a side road to the left leading up into the hills. About a mile south-east of the village was Doddiscombe Farm, a farm mentioned in the Domesday Book.

In January 1941 I walked with father to Shillingford and measured the distance with a pedometer. We walked ten miles and visited two farms and a cottage, the cottage snug and cosy, the doubtless more prosperous farms bleak with large stone-flagged floors, and only a smouldering log on the wide open fireplace.

Clayhanger church is built of a hard grey limestone and is dedicated to St. Peter. There is a tall Devon tower at the west end with two buttresses. Going through the wooden farm gate to the churchyard, the west end is directly in front and has a high arched narrow window in the lower storey. The next storey is blank with a window in the south, and the top belfrey has narrow slatted windows on every side in which hang three bells. The door is in the south through a round arched porch. Either side are narrow steeply arched windows. The roof is of slate tiles with a little decoration along the top.

Inside there is a nave leading up to a narrower and lower chancel. At the entrance to the chancel is the remains of a 15th. century wooden screen. The font at the west end dates from the early 13th. century. By far the most interesting features of the church are the original pews, early 16th. century dark oak pews with end carvings. We sat on the left near the front and across from us was a large carved pew end of the sun god complete with face. On the floor are ancient slabs dating from the early 16th. century onwards of the Nutcombe family, former squires. The Victorians restored the church between 1879 and 1881 fortunately not changing the lovely old pews for pine. Miss Widlake used to read the lessons at Matins. On the altar was a large and heavy brass cross flanked by two heavy brass vases. These were very tall and very narrow, ornamented at the top. They had been made from shell cases from the first world war. When we cleaned the brass we could hardly lift them down, and when we tried to arrange flowers in them they would only stand straight in stiff bunches. The flowers had to be immensely long in order to appear at all at the top of the vase.

While we were there father and mother made carpets for the chancel. Father made a wide red hooked rug for the aisle between the choir pews, and mother made gros-point tapestry kneelers for the altar rail.

Father was very fortunate with regard to congregations. Every Sunday

St. Peter's Church, Clayhanger.

Church and cottages.

during term time he could count on thirty or so from the rectory, the girls walking up the hill in crocodile in their green coats and velour hats in winter, or blazers and panamas in summer. They sat in a block in the pews on the right hand side. Apart from them there was a small devoted congregation, farmers and labourers and their wives and children. The manor house did not attend church. Mr. Williams who was there when we went was not a church goer, and his successor was a Roman Catholic. One of the churchwardens, Mr. Elworthy, was a retired farmer. The other was a retired blacksmith, Mr. Carr, who lived at the old smithy near Bonny Cross. There was also a verger and sexton, Mr. Fred Curtis, a farm labourer from South Hele Farm along Featherbed Lane. He had ten or eleven children and brought them up on a farm labourer's wage plus six shillings a week for acting as verger.

On 21st. March 1943 I was confirmed in St. Peter's Church, Clayhanger, by Curzon, Bishop of Exeter, with some of the girls. They wore their green tussore dresses and mother made one for me, so that we were all dressed alike. Afterwards we had our photograph taken on the front lawn.

The communion plate was silver, dated 1572, a large heavy chalice and paten. It was in its original thick dark leather container with leather handle. Father kept it under his bed, and carried it up to church on Sundays. He cut up the bread for Holy Communion into small squares at home. At Harvest Festival he used the harvest loaf which was laid on the altar.

The registers of the church were very ancient. The burial register is among the earliest in the country, dating from 1532, and being complete from the autumn of that year, well kept and in good condition. This is the earliest possible date for records to exist. It was in 1532 that Thomas Cromwell, the Chancellor of Henry VIII, proposed the keeping of parochial records of births, marriages and deaths, and therefore some churches still have records dating from then, Clayhanger being one of only four in Devon to have such early records. The registers were also kept at home, and we were sometimes allowed to look at them if father was making an entry. Until the war all the registers were kept by the vicar or rector either in the church or at home, but now many are kept in the county archives. This is a pity in many ways as it means that the records are no longer as accessible as they used to be.

Father was rector of Clayhanger and perpetual curate of Petton. He was instituted to the Chapelry of Petton in Exeter on 26th. November 1939. Tulliedeigh Ogilvey was with us and drove father to Exeter. In those days one paid legal fees on one's institution to a livivg, and father was surprised at the large amount for his institution to Petton Chapel, £42 13s. 4d. The stipend at Petton was £90 per year at that time! The fee was six months salary! These fees have now been abolished.

The chapel at Petton was dedicated to St. Petroc, a west country saint; and the name of the hamlet a Roman corruption of Petroc's town. It was possibly the home of an anchorite of that name who had a tiny chapel and congregation there. There had been an old church there, but it was completely rebuilt by the Victorians in 1847. It is a small chapel with a single bell tower and a rose window in the west end. The windows were plain glass, a plain rounded font, and simple pews and furnishings. The church was white-washed inside. The service there was usually at 3.30 p.m., and father would walk either round by the road, two and a half miles, in very wet weather, or across the fields of Nutcombe Manor, passing in front of the house. I often walked with him. Occasionally there would be a bull in one of the fields, a large and fearsome looking animal, and we would go hurriedly round the edge, and back along the road. The farmer told us that bulls were quite safe in fields full of cows, but we did not wish to put him to the test.

Harvest Festival was a great occasion at Petton, and we were always amazed at the number of people who turned up on the Saturday to decorate the church lavishly with masses of farm and garden produce. This was a real social occasion, and all the women gathered from the local farms and cottages to have a good talk as well as to work. The roof was lifted at the service the following day, with all the extra male voices raised in the harvest hymns. The harvest there was always early, mid-September, either the second or third Sunday.

We only heard the bells for the first few months, as in 1940 bells ceased to be rung except in case of an emergency, such as invasion.

Venn Cross was a few scattered farms and cottages round a cross roads across the main Taunton-Barnstable road, and the station, which took its name from the cross roads.

There was only one charity in Clayhanger, which was administered by the rector and two wardens, who were the trustees. It was the Sayer's Bread Charity, and dated from 1699. It was a land charge of thirty shillings a year levied on the Gamlin's Farm, a farm between Venn Cross and Petton, south of the road. The trustees wrote annually for it, and at Christmas it was distributed in the form of bread to old people in the parish. One year father suggested that as the old people were no longer short of bread they should have cake instead as a treat. This was greeted by a shocked silence. And rightly so. The benefactor of long ago wanted them to have bread. Many of the remote villages and hamlets of our country have ancient charities created to bring a little happiness into the lives of the old and needy at Christmas, and although they may have no longer needed it, they were pleased to receive it, and to be remembered annually in this way.

Chapter 9.   ANIMALS

Skerryvore

> My house, I say. But hark to the sunny doves
> That make my roof the arena of their loves,
> That gyre about the gable all day long
> And fill the chimneys with their murmurous song;
> Our house, they say; and mine, the cat declares,
> And spreads his golden fleece upon the chairs;
> And mine, the dog, and rises stiff with wrath
> If any alien foot profane the path.
> So, too, the buck that trimmed my terraces,
> Our whilome gardener, called the garden his;
> Who now, deposed, surveys my plain abode
> And his late kingdom, only from the road.
>   R. L. Stevenson.

When we went to Clayhanger in 1939, we were delighted to be in the heart of the country, and devoted ourselves to the study of the countryside and its life, large and small. Father bought us the books in the Observer series, British Birds, Wild Flowers, Butterflies, Trees and Shrubs, and British Wild Animals, useful little books which could be slipped into the pocket. I still have them and use them.

We were not at all scientific in our study of the countryside. Everything, large or small, common or rare was of interest, and everything portable was carried home, and put in the museum; tattered old birds' nests, broken pieces of birds eggs dropped from nests, a dozen blue jay's feathers found in a clump one day, and, most precious of all, the sloughed-off skin of a grass snake. It was crumbling and unrecognizable by the time we got it home, a mouldering brown fragile skin, but proudly labelled 'snake', and put on one of the shelves.

Every year we had a nature calendar, a page for every month with pictures and poems suitable to the time of year, and on the back, a little square for each day to record the weather pictorially, and a few lines to record items of special interest. Every January I made a New Year's resolution to keep this nature diary through the year, but never succeeded in getting beyond April. After the first few days of each month the weather was no longer recorded, and after May's sad entry 'Forgot what did or saw', no further attempt was made until the following January.

The first wild life we began to see in Devon was stream life. All our spare time the first few months was spent wading upstream from the bottom of the drive along various small tributaries. Certainly we never saw

Nipper's puppies.
Roderick with bow.

Puppies and Miss Matty.

Marion with Rex,
Nipper and Harry.

Nipper in bath.

anything very large. The stream was tiny and too far from the Exe to produce a salmon or trout. There was nothing larger than a minnow in the fish line. On 9th. March 1940 in a still pool we found masses of frog spawn, and rushed home for a bucket. We kept it in an old tin bath in the courtyard, and eventually it changed into tadpoles which began to grow legs. We never actually saw the final frogs. They must have jumped away in the night back to the stream. Occasionally we saw a newt, and one red letter day in the Barle, a stickle-back, much smaller than the illustration in Jeremy Fisher had led us to believe it would be. In the summer radiant dragonflies hovered over the streams with their transparent wings, and the surface of the water was covered with scurrying water boatmen.

In the willow tree on the island in the pond at the bottom of the garden lived a kingfisher, very shy. We occasionally saw the bluegreen flash of his wings as he swooped down over the water to catch a tiny fish. In the summer he seemed to eat dragonflies and insects as well, catching them in his beak as he skimmed down to the water. Once further down stream beyond the watersplash we found a kingfisher's nest, filled with eight large whitish eggs, almost an inch long. It was a messy nest, really a hollow scooped out in the damp bank of the stream and lined or littered with bits of twig and moss, and dried fish bones. We went back several times to see the eggs but did not see them hatch out.

Moorhens were common and in the spring we would see the young swimming with their mothers along the streams. Occasionally a heron standing on the bank or flying to his high nest in the heronry dowm towards Petton. The fields after ploughing were filled with flocks of lapwings with their tufted heads. Walking along the lanes we would see all the common hedge birds. A pair of greenfinches nested year after year in the hedge to the east of the house, very bravely because of the cats.

We usually recorded the arrival of the swallows, the earliest being 23rd. February 1941, very early, in a mild winter. We were too young to write to the Times! Father would tell us when the first cuckoo had been heard, and we would prick up our ears. It was days before we heard one. The earliest we heard it was 10th. April 1943, a date the real cuckoo lover would scorn to record. In 1943 the swallow failed to arrive. March and April came and went. No swallow. That year as far as I know the swallow did not reach our shores. We put it down to the fighting in north Africa. The fighting was right across the flight path of the swallow, and they were perhaps afraid to cross it, hearing or feeling the vibrations of the gunfire in the air. We awaited them anxiously in 1944 and all was well.

They came.

In 1943 I became a subscriber to a modest duplicated nature periodical of some four sheets per issue, entitled ' Countryside Calling'. In Vol.1 no.4 I saw my name in print under the proud heading 'Naturalists' Experiences'. 'Miss Drew of Tiverton writes, 'All this summer we have had two little sparrow friends. When we are at tea under the verandah, they come up to within a few feet of where we are sitting, and tweet until we throw them food. At the side of the house there was a house martin's nest. The sparrows pushed the martins out of the nest and took it for their own. The ruffled martins built another nest joined on to their old one''.

We never collected birds' eggs. We pored over bird books and found that this was considered reprehensible, and we anxious to do what was right, having a high regard for the printed word. But we used to look in nests. And watch the communal activity of the rooks engaged in repairing their nests in a slapdash fashion chatting loudly all the while. Once we saw, near Porlock by the sea a crowd of puffins, for the first time.

We were fortunate as children always to have plenty of books. Whenever we showed sn interest in any subject we were provided with books about it. For my birthday in 1940 I was given 'A Bird in the Bush', by E.Hilton Young, illustrated by Peter Scott in colour and black and white sketches. This inspired us to attempt to illustrate our own efforts, usually rather unintelligible to other people, but satisfying to us. Then the following year I had 'Wild Chorus' and 'Morning Flight' by Peter Scott. They were the most wonderful and largest books I ever received, and I have them still.

We used to collect caterpillars in the autumn and keep them in boxes filled with cabbage leaves. In due course they would turn into crysalids and we put them in match boxes. But that was the end of it. We would let them out in the spring, but they never progressed any further. No moth or butterfly ever emerged to fly away.

There was one winged creature we were not fond of, the bat. Bats were the one drawnback to coming home from school after dark. As soon as dusk fell, the sky seemed to be thick with them swooping down over the road and hedges. We were scared of them getting entangled in our hair, although we had never actually heard of this happening. For two years I had my hair long, and although it was in pigtails on school days, I used to tuck them into my gaberdene for safety. One dreadful night I woke up to hear a bat swooping round my room. It had flown in and was unable to find the way out. I lit my candle, but hastily put it out as the bat flew towards the light. Then I dashed for the door and spent the rest of the night in the large dormitory. In the morning we searched high and low for it, expecting to find it hanging upside down under the bed. But it was gone. Years later it happened again, so it is unfortunately not a unique occurence.

We were always interested in farm animal life. In those days the hens were free and happy scratching in the yards. Our own hens had a huge grassy run and warm huts with straw-filled nesting boxes. Apart from the smell I liked the feel of warm hen when we were collecting the eggs. Occasionally a broody hen would give a sharp peck. Several farmers kept guinea fowl and bantams, and we had their eggs. We also ate guinea fowl when we could get it. When the hens grew too old to lay, mother boiled the with vegetables. Poultry had a much more delicious and gamier flavour than the white and tasteless meat from the batteries of today. In the spring I used to go with mother to a farm where we would buy a dozen or more day-old chicks, at 1d. per chick. We would take them home in a box and give them to a broody hen who would recive them raptuously.

The fields of Devon are filled with sheep and cattle. Early in December we used to look out for the first lamb, and the earliest one we saw was 5th. December 1940. January produced the greatest number of lambs, and the shepherds were out all night in the fields with their flocks. There were small enclosures with a lean-to hut at one end. Others were erected in a sheltered corner of the field out of bales of straw and hay, to make a snug enclosure. There were always sheep in the field I crossed near Venn Cross to the station, by Woodlands Farm, and there often seemed to be a bottlefed lamb who followed hopefully, butting my legs.

Many fields were filled with dairy cattle, the most common being Jerseys, Guernseys and Red Devons. Every tiny field and water meadow seemed to have its cows, only the steeper fields being kept for sheep. Every day the milk lorries came round collecting the churns from outside the farm, beside the road. Most of the milking was done by hand as there was no electricity, and not all farmers had generators. Larger farms had a cowman, smaller ones relied on their families to milk. It was a much more laborious business than it is today. There were also herds of heifers and bullocks, ususally separate. We soon got used to them galumphing towards us when we entered their field. The young animals were always curious about strangers, and it broke the monotony to frolic about in pretended panic. We used to walk calmly across the field with all the herd pushing and shoving behind, and the front ones breathing heavily down our necks. Our visitors were not always so sanguine, and occasionally had to be forcibly restrained from haring off in headlong panic, particularly if they were being pursued by bullocks.

Once during the war foot and mouth disease broke out, and precautions were taken to prevent it spreading. Farms which were attacked had to destroy the healthy as well as the sick animals, and sheep and cattle were decimated. Farms free of the disease set up barriers of disinfectant, through which tractors and feet had to go. The only good result was that one winter there was plenty of meat to be had.

There was one poor farmer, a small holder with a ramshackle farm. He was new to the district and came to rear pigs. One hefty pig used to regularly break into our vegetable garden to eat the cabbages. No one saw him, only the evidence he left behind of hoof prints and mangled plants. One morning father got up early and caught the offender red handed. He rushed at it shouting furiously, but porker stood his ground. He waited for father to approach and then charged him, and he was forced to flee ignominiously from his own garden. He rang the farmer in a rage, and two men appeared rather gingerly, and carted the pig off. We had no more trouble after that. However, one day we were woken by sounds of a clog dance on the verandah, and there was a large cart horse who had leapt out of an adjacent field. He pranced all over the lawn, and although he didn't eat anything the large holes he left in the soft turf took weeks to recover.

Other unexpected visitors were the hunt. (It closed for the duration of the war in 1940). Shortly after we arrived we heard a tally-ho! and streaming up the drive were hounds and horses following a fox who had a couple of hundred yards start into the field. Harry and I rushed out. The hounds streamed under the fence, but we had to open the small gate into the field to let the horses through. They had come up the drive so there was no damage done to the garden that time.

Whenever we went into the wooded valleys round Dulverton and along the Barle and Exe valleys deep in the moors, we used to see deer, either in pairs or small herds, the Red Deer of Exmoor. They were off in a flash when our scent reached them. Also on the moor were herds of wild and shaggy ponies. During the war much of the edge of the moor was taken into cultivation; and the sides and heads of the deep valleys were enclosed in fields and farmed. Sheep and cattle were put to graze on the moor, and the ferns and heather retreated.

Often we saw grass snakes. Devon seems rife with small summer snakes in the damp hollows. Several times we saw adders, and once one ventured right to the house. Hugh, a brave boy, bashed it on the head with his cricket bat, killing it instantly, and left its writhing body on the verandah. We were fascinated and repelled, and sorry it was dead although we feared it living.

We always had a number of pets living with us, and they tended to increase in number. When we arrived in 1939 we brought with us Timothy Titus, Timmy, a Blue Persian. He had been born on a farm in east Kent, and was glad to return to country living. He was born in 1932 and came as a kitten to us in Deal. He was fed from the start on liver and lights. In those days a 'pennorth of lights' went a long way, and a cat could be kept in luxury on 6d. per week. In 1937 the man next door dug an ornamental pond and stocked it with one hundred goldfish. These rapidly decreased in number, and we were embarrased when they appeared on our back doorstep as gifts for us. We were alarmed whem seven appeared in rapid succession, followed by the bedraggled fisher who had fallen in. While we were in Deal father wrote a poem to him.

To Blue Persian

Timmy, you understanding little beast;
Your love may be,
Nay, certainly
Is cupboard - but its genuine at least.

Appetite satisfied - you play and stretch
Just at your ease;
Do as you please
With children, neighbours, birds and mice-you wretch!

In summer you lie basking in the sun,
Lazy, blinking,
Mind unthinking,
Peaceful, contented; after all your fun.

The children love to tease and play with you;
You purr and bite
With much delight;
Its joy to them whatever you may do.

At night its best of all, for there you lie,
Outstretched, asleep,
Sometimes - a peep
Of eyelid shows - but otherwise you die.

Then mistress starts the brush and comb to wield
On your rich fur;
And what a rare
Tussle begins - she chuckles - you must yield.

Timmy travelled with us to Cambridge where he hunted over Parker's Piece, outside our lodging. Then to St. Helen's, where he had only a small garden. But this backed on to a large park with a lake. So he was able to continue his fishing. The outbreak of war meant the disappearance of liver and lights from his menu. Also, a big industrial town meant endless washing, a ceaseless battle against soot. So he, too, was pleased with the move to Devon, at the age of seven. He was the only really keen hunter and fisher amongst us, and came into his element there.

Timmy systematically set out to rid the house and garden of small rodents, mice, rats, shrews and voles. Then he turned his attention to the fields. These were stocked with rabbits. Young rabbit became his favourite delicacy. He used to lie in wait at a burrow until an unsuspecting young rabbit emerged. If very hungry he would devour it on the spot, and come staggering home with sides bulging, to sleep flat out for hours. But mostly he carried his prey home. He had one particular place in which he liked to eat, the hedge east of the house. This was a thick high hedge, and he made a tunnel right through, with a hollow place in the middle to dine. He dumped the rabbit there, and devoured it whole. Nothing remained except the smell. Rex and Matty, the other cats would station themselves hopefully at either side of the tunnel, but if they ventured a paw inside they would be warned with a growl, and if they went too far, the fur would fly. After his meal he would emerge grunting and bloated, and they would rusah in to lick the smell.

All these hunting activities were not harmless. There were other poachers after rabbits, and often burrows were netted and traps were set along rabbit runs. Several times Timmy came home with a swollen torn paw, wrenched from a trap. Once he came home dragging the trap behind him, and once he didn't come home at all. The next day we called anxiously all round the garden and neighbouring fields. We heard faint and pitiful cries, and found him with his head in a barbed wire noose, pressed into the mud, almost dead. We carried him carefully home, after destroying the vicious trap, and he lay limp beside the fire. Next day he managed some warm milk, and gradually recovered. Fortunately, the vicious traps and nooses are now gone, perhaps because of myxomatosis, perhaps for humanitarian reasons, or perhaps because the labourer now gets a decent wage. Probably all three. The rabbit is back in our fields, but let us hope the trap never returns.

Timmy was an outdoor cat, out in all weathers, except snow which he deplored. He patted it and sniffed it, and sneezed it out, and retired indoors. Only once I remember him after prolonged snow, out in it, taking large strides and shaking it off disdainfully, in February 1941. He spent his old age in Berkshire, living to fifteen. When he died, we planted an almond tree in his memory, and on it nailed a small plaque 'Timmy Titus, Blue Persian, 1932 - 1947'. The tree grew large and bore copious fruit, keeping his memory fresh and green.

The other cats were Matty and Rex. Rex was an evacuee. He came with the school, and seemed to belong to them all. He was reputed to have been the mascot of the Royal Marines in Walmer, his home town. He had been born in the marines barracks, and given to Miss Widlake. He arrived in a cat basket and was received very suspiciously by Timmy. He had an indeterminate ancestry. He was mainly white with blotches of a variety of hues, tabby and tortoiseshell over his flanks and face, a real hotchpotch ragbag of cat. He was larger than Timmy, and fierce when he arrived. Timmy soon convinced him who was resident chief cat, and he accepted his secondary position with a few grumbles. His favourite indoor place was the small sitting-room, where he knew he was the favourite of the girls. He was not much of a hunter, being content with the ample meals provided.

When we had been a few months in Clayhanger we were offered a charming black and white kitten alleged to be male. We realized soon enough she wasn't, but had fallen for her endearing ways, and kept her. We called her Miss Matty. Her main colour was black, but she had four white paws, white whiskers and a white dicky. Her chief occupation was washing. Having completed her own toilet, she began on Timmy and Rex. They usually allowed her to wash them, unless she forgot herself and trod on them to reach a distant corner, and then she was growled off. However, she was quite undaunted, and began on the dogs who were much more tolerant. Once Miss Widlake picked up her fur coat to put it on, but dropped it with a shudder. It was damp. Matty had more or less washed the whole coat!

Matty had two favourite places in the house. As a tiny kitten she had curled up in the big brass bowl that stood on the wooden linen chest on the upstairs landing in front of the south facing window. When the sun shone it warmed the bowl, and sometimes her fur grew so hot it stuck to her damply. Cats can stand a great deal of warmth, but sometimes she emerged dazed and limp with heat exhaustion. When she grew too big for the bowl, she would drape herself elegantly round it to soak up the warmth. Once there was a watch glass in the bowl on top of some papers, and the sun shining through the window set them alight. This started a craze for lighting fires without matches. We all carried a small piece of glass and paper in our pockets in case a fire was needed suddenly.

Another place Matty liked to sit on was on the round newel post at the foot of the stairs, so that her black and white fur was shown off against the warm polished wood of the banisters. This was also a convenient place for stroking by anyone using the telephone, which stood on the table at the foot of the stairs.

Later, inevitably, kittens arrived. We would keep one and harden our hearts about the others. As we were all soft about kittens father paid a boy to take them away. Getting a good home for the remaining kitten was always an anxious task, and several times I took one hopefully to school in a box to unload on an unsuspecting, susceptible friend.

We have only one photo of Matty, taken when a tiny kitten with Nipper's three puppies. She was quite impossible to photograph. As soon as anyone with a camera appeared she hared off to some dark safe place, and watched with big eyes from an impossible cranny. However quietly one stalked her, like all cats she slept with one ear open and seemed to sense the arrival of a camera. Perhaps she had seen a rabbit shot and thought it was a gun. She was so obviously terrified, even when held, that we gave up the attempt.

In March 1940 father was given a golden retriever, a female, the smallest in the litter. 'What do you call her?' he asked. 'We calls her the nipper'. So 'The Nipper' she remained, although she grew to be a large dog, and eventually topped the scales at six stone. On arrival Timmy showed her her place clearly and forever - inferior to that of the cats, and Nipper took it humbly. She had a vast tin food bowl, filled to the brim at tea-time. Timmy was sometimes there, and she stood aside for him to take a tasty morsel, slobbering anxiously the while. Then she would fall on the food and it was gone in a flash. She had a large basket in the kitchen which grew with her, bulging out all round. It had an old blanket inside, and occasionally Timmy, and sometimes all three cats would snuggle down in it. Then she would wait rather mournfully on the cold tiles for them to move.

Nipper was father's dog, although she was devoted to all the family, and welcomed the arrival of the girls raptuously. Father used to take her visiting every afternoon, and always on Sunday to Petton. She would spend the service lying in the vestry, occasionally joining in the hymns with a mournful howl. She carried father's walking stick proudly, to save him. But unfortunately she was so far ahead as a rule, that when she got tired of it and dropped it, we couldn't always find it. Being a tidy dog she didn't leave it in the road but in the long grass of the bank. She lost a silver-handled stick and a polished carved mahogany with a bull dog's head, which he had inherited. After that father or Nipper just carried an ordinary stick of no value.

When there was no other walk in the offing Nipper joined the girls.

There used to be two walks, a long one for the older girls and a short walk for the rest. Although she loved long walks, Nipper always chose to go with the small children, looking upon herself as their guardian, rounding them up periodically like a sheep dog. She would dash off ahead for a run, then come back to supervise.

On very long walks Nipper occasionally got left behind. She would start off full of bounce, making quite unnecessary forays into the adjacent countryside. Then after eight or nine miles she would begin to flag. She sat down hopefully and let us all disappear into the distance before getting up and limping after. Once when we had been a long walk on Exmoor, we returned by train from Morebath. In the rush to get everyone on the train she was left behind in the waiting room. No once noticed until we were home, and none of us could remember when we had seen her last. Then the station master rang and asked us to come and remove our fierce dog! She was so frightened at being left that she would let no one approach. It was easier said than done to retrieve her from six miles away. We persuaded the station master that it would be quite safe to put her on the next train which we would meet at Venn Cross. This he did and eventually she was home again late at night. She took care not to let it happen again, and was always the first on the platform panting to be off when the train arrived.

Unlike the cats Nipper loved the snow and rolled about in it, snuffling it with her nose. She was eager to join in any snow fight going on and bounced on anyone wallowing on the ground, covering them with warm wet licks. She also loved the sea and would swim far out to retrieve sticks and balls. So it was strange that she didn't like baths. As soon as the galvanized iron bath appeared she slunk off, only to be hauled back. Three people were needed to heave her in and soap her down. Once in, all bounce left her. She drooped, the picture of woe and oppression, dripping with soapsuds. We poured a bucket over her to rinse it off and then she rushed off to shake herself all over anyone nearby. The washers wore protective clothing and wellingtons, but were still pretty soaking wet at the end. We only bathed her a few times when she was particularly smelly after rolling in a dead sheep carcase.

Christmas 1941 saw Nipper in disgrace. She was really old enough by then to know better. We had seven girls and two staff with us that Christmas and mother had roasted a huge turkey. It was fortunate that we had all eaten largely, for it was the last time we tasted turkey that Christmas. Someone had staggered out with the remains of the feast to the kitchen and dumped them on the table. We had all gathered round the fire in the lounge to eat our Christmas sweets for which we had saved our rations and to gloat over Christmas gifts. I was deep in one of the eight books I had received (a record number). About three we decided to wash up before going for a walk. What a disaster met our eyes in the kitchen! Nothing remained of the turkey. One replete dog lay stretched out in the middle of the floor surrounded by mangled bones and pieces of stuffing. We talked seriously about giving her away. Even more so on the morrow when we had only roast potatoes and vegetables for lunch, instead of our delicious cold bird. Even Harry and I felt disagreeable towards her, and she knew she was beyond the pale this time, as she could usually count on us to take her part. It was the last time we left temptation in her way.

Nipper had one litter of puppies, ten in all, nine golden and one black. We kept three, the black and two others. The black puppy was given to a policeman and trained as a police dog. One golden puppy was given away in the village, and the other was given to Jane Bayly. She called him Dusty, and he lived with us for three years until Jane went away to be a land girl, and took him with her. Dusty and Nipper were inseparable, and got up to all kinds of mischief together.

Nipper was a simple dog. Her one trick was to give her paw. In the morning this meant 'hello again', at meal times 'may I have some too?' On one of my rare stays away from home in early spring 1941, Harry wrote me about the animals: 'We have had som more snow hear but only a light fall. We have been teaching Nipper som tricks but she wont understand. We will be seeing you on fryday. With best wishes from Harry D. P.S. Timmy is well but Rex has been cort in a trap but is all right now.'

Nipper lived to be ten and died in Berkshire. We left Matty behind with Winnie Tucker, but always regretted leaving her. Timmy also missed her as he had to wash himself in future. He lived on into old age and accepted Nipper's successor, a black labrador.

Lorna Doone Farm, Malmesmead.

Bridge at Malmesmead.

Miss Ward, Mrs Peerless, Miss Widlake, father and mother.

Chapter 10   OUTINGS AND HOLIDAYS

                              Devon Streams

                    Okement and Erme and Avon,
                    Exe and his ruffled shallows,
                    I could cry as I think of those rivers
                    That knew my morning dreams;
                    The weir by Tavistock at evening
                    When the circling woods were purple,
                    And the Lowman in spring with the Lent-lilies,
                    And the little moorland streams.

                                            Sir John Squire.

There were many drawbacks both from the point of view of the girls and ourselves to the Rectory being used as a school. It was built as a private house for a large family, but not quite so large. There were naturally no proper classroom facilities and no provision for games. There was no school nearby who could offer to share playing fields. In summer a tennis net was put up on the lawn, but as there were no surrounding nets time was wasted fetching the ball from the field below. The west lawn was devoted to croquet and clock golf - hardly a substitute for school games. Every afternoon rain or fine, two walks set off after lunch, short for the smaller children, long for the older. The standard long walk was up the hill to Bonny Cross, along Featherbed Lane, over Combe Downs road tom Venn Cross and back over Well Hayes Hill. This was only about three miles but over hills varying rapidly from 550 feet to 870, and taking an hour.

On Saturdays we went further afield - sometimes to Ashbrittle along winding lanes, stopping at the bakery for floury buns fresh from the oven. It was a pleasure to walk along the narrow lanes in wartime. There was virtually no traffic. Private cares had more or less disappeared, and essential traffice had only a tiny petrol ration, so one could enjoy country roads in peace.

Most of us were keen on wild flowers and were making collections of pressed flowers. Devon was an ideal spot for this with its many rare species of orchids and others. We were of course, catholic in our tastes, collecting everything however common. One year, 1943, we were systematic in our collections and wrote short accounts of where we found our flowers and their environment. We were rather rough and ready in our classification, labelling plants under five main headings, hedge top, hedge bank, hedge battom, woodland, and swampland. That year we collected thirty two different kinds of wild flower.

The earliest of the 1943 collection was actually 13th. December 1942, and was the hazel catkin. It was a very mild winter and 20th. December saw the flowering currant in leaf. The pussy willow was out on 15th. January and also the elm leaves. In February the larch was in leaf, and 3rd. February the blackthorn in flower (very early). The horsechestnut came into leaf 29th. March, and into flower 27th. April. All the blossom was early that year.

Some of the hedges on top of banks in Devon are very old, probably hundreds of years old. The spindle bush which is usually the last to establish itself in a hedge, was common along the lanes in the hedges, and we used to pick the pink blossom for harvest festival.

The flowers were also early in 1943, the periwinkle appearing just before Christmas, the crocus 9th. January, the wild strawberry 13th., and the primrose on 21st. January the earliest I have ever found it. The first week of March saw red campion, stitchwort, dead nettle and wild daffodil, and the first week of April, the kingcup, bluebell, buttercup and ladies smock among others. We found the first orchid, the early purple orchis on 10th. April, and the pyramidal orchis on 23rd. April. The last week in April we picked and ate wild strawberries. A really mild winter and spring, very helpful from the clothing and food point of viiew, as everything was getting scarcer the fourth winter of the war.

Other Saturday walks we took were over the top of the hill south of us to Huntsham in a wooded valley. The stream which rose in the Huntsham parish was the Lowman, which formed a small lake east of the village, which we passed. It ran north through a fairly steep valley to the village of Uplowman on the edge of the wider valley in which lies Tiverton. Tiverton is at the junction of the Exe and Lowman rivers, and also the Great Western Canal. This canal links the Exe and the Tone, flowing from the Tone above Wellington, about 250 feet up, through Sampford Peverell and Halberton before reaching Tiverton, slightly lower at 220 feet, in a valley some three miles wide. We had to carry a picnic with us to Huntsham as there was no bakery in the village. Sometimes we set off after lunch and walked across the fields to Petton, across the main road and then up the Batherm valley which runs through steep wooded slopes between Haddon Hill and the Brendon Hills. From Batherm Bridge we could go east towards Chipstable and then over Shute Hill to Venn Cross and home. This was a walk of about seven miles and entailed climbing up to 950 feet over Shute Hill.

Sometimes for a treat we went to Waterrow. We used to walk along a back road behind Venn Cross to avoid the main road. This road plunged down the hillside above Waterrow in one of the steepest descents I know, one in four. At the bottom was Rock Inn and the tiny upper Tone in its steep wooded valley. Waterrow clings to the side of the valley, a few cottages with steep gardens and overhanging woods with the swift stream below and the main road to Taunton hugging the stream. It is here that the railway makes a wide detour to the south to avoid an impossible gradient. A few hundred yards along the main road was a modest teaplace, the front room of a cottage. Here we had the most delicious homemade teas with two boiled eggs each, bread and butter and homemade jam and cake, a real treat in wartime. A bus ran past at six from Wiveliscombe and we took it as far as Venn Cross.

Sometimes in very hot weather we didn't go a long walk, but carried our picnic tea into one of the nearby woods, a favourite being Quarry Wood across the glebe meadow and stream. We were fascinated by the quarry and never tired of carrying pieces of its striped rock home to add to our collection. Or to Nutcombe Copse, the largest wood, with leafy glades and bridle tracks. Most of the younger ones under twelve wanted to play at Robin Hood, and we would in rather a desultory way. But the main group of us were at the age of chivalry and we always carried our swords with us on short walks. Mostly we were knights of the round table setting out for adventures. We would have several battles on the way, and stop at the church on the way home for an imaginary vigil. I say imaginary, for we never actually went in to keep the vigil, but just paused to imagine it, before battling on. We could never find out anything at all about the knights. They had vanished without a trace as if they had never been.

Some of our expeditions were in search of food. In August and September we went blackberrying on every possible occasion, taking a picnic, and coming home with anything from five to twenty pounds for mother to bottle and jam. When the sugar was gone mother would bottle them. There were no domestic freezers in those days, and we didn't have a pressure cooker, so it was a wearisome business. We could help her fill the jars, and then they were boiled for hours in the preserving pan or baked in the oven over the oil stove. It was a much more hit abd miss affair in those days with glass tops and rubber rings. In the morning we would anxiously test them to see if they had 'taken'. Sometimes they all had, but usually one at least had failed to seal, and had to be done again or else eaten.

Blackberries were our most valuable country crop, but we also picked crab applles for jelly, and every year we made one or two expeditions for whortleberries. We called them bilberries, and they are known in various parts of the country as blueberries, whinberries or blaeberries, but in Devon we went over the the local name of 'whorts'. The nearest place these grew was in the Haddon and Heydon hills just north of Venn Cross, and now part of the Exmoor National Park area. It was a whole days walk for the whortleberries. In the Heydon hills we used to walk to Huish Champflower, a remote village in the upper Tone valley. We set off after breakfast carrying an enormous picnic, Nigger running on ahead with her stick. First to Venn Cross and over Shute Hill. From there on the country was bare and empty, just a few farms in the valleys. The road gradually rose to the top of Heydon Hill, climbing to over 1100 feet. The top was covered with patches of moorland and the valleys were wooded, having been planted with mixed woodland. We used to start to pick here. What a slow business picking whorts. I don't ever remember picking more than seven pounds all fifteen of us. But at least one can sit down to pick. The berries grew in clumps - one can sit on a bouncy hummock and pick all round before moving on. The best time was early August for the big juicy ones. After picking we would walk into the tiny village of Huish Champflower to see the church with its very high tower dominating the skyline. Then to eat our lunch in the sun and to play on the moor. Although we were tired at the end of the day, the return seemed much quicker, being mainly downhill. We sometimes went straight down the Tone valley, scrambling down through the woods between Washbottle Bridge and Wadham Farm, along a narrow track down to Waterrow for the bus. It was about two miles through the woods, very steep-sided, but our packs were empty and we rushed through. All except Nipper who was flagging by this time. Once we tried to make her carry a basket of provisions in her mouth instead of the stick, but she soon dropped it. Another time we fixed up a little wheeled cart and harnessed her to it like a sledge dog. But she was not amused and just lay down mournfully between the shafts.

When we walked over Haddon Hill we took the train to Morebath Junction Halt and walked up the hill to the top, 1100 feet, and about four miles from Morebath. From the top there is a wonderful view to the west across the river Exe deep in its woods, to Exmoor beyond. We walked as far as Skilgate where we picniced above the village, then down to the Batherm valley and back through Petton.

Several times we made expeditions into Exmoor. Clayhanger is only about six miles from the moor, and we were conscious of its presence in the distance. Nowadays this would be an easy Saturday afternoon outing by car. But there were no car drives for pleasure during the war, and it was an all day outing for us by train and on foot. Several times we went to

Tarr Steps. It was the first long walk we did in Devon, and the longest walk Harry and I had ever done. The first time we went was 15th. June 1940 just after the school arrived. We went with some of the older girls and took the train to Brushford, the station for Dulverton, some two miles out of the small town. We walked along beside the river Barle in its steeply wooded banks. On the right was Pixton Park, the manor house of Dulverton in its huge wooded grounds covering the whole of Pixton Hill overlooking the town in the distance. Dulverton is right on the edge of the moor, and the market for south-east Exmoor, in a very beautiful situation. There was an enormous very old sycamore tree beside the church. We left the town and continued along the road which hugs the left bank of the Barle, whose valley gradually steepens. The river here is about 500 feet up and the wooded banks on either side climb very steeply to over 1000 feet. This is a very ancient part of the country. The higher slopes are covered with barrows and earthworks. The river itself is overlooked by several castles, not the romantic stone built castles of Wales, but ancient earthworks in commanding positions. Almost every swing of the river was overlooked by a defensive position, Oldberry Castle, Mounsey and Brewers' Castles all being within a few miles of Dulverton.
Tarr Steps are about six miles upstream from Dulverton. The road leaves the river after two miles or so, and goes inland over the hill, and is one of the roads across the moor to the coast. We crossed the river where we left the road and continued along a footpath through the lovely woods. The river is wide and shallow and fairly swift. The path was a few feet above on the steep hillside. Mary Peerless and I were in front, and rounding a corner were lucky enough to see a pair of red deer drinking. We stopped, but they were off in a flash. The red deer are very timid, and often one can cross the moor without seeing any, unlike the friendly ponies. It is a very winding path along the river. About a mile before the steps it joins a narrow country lane which leads down to cross the river. Tarr Steps are a very ancient crossing place and their origin iis long forgotten. At the time we first went we believed them to be prehistoric, used by the men who built the earthworks that cover the moor and who are buried in the barrows. They are on the line of a very early route across the moor from south-east to north-west with an intersection with the east-west route at Exford in the centre of the moor. The steps are an elaborate form of stepping stones, huge oblong flattish stones supported on other stones standing upright in the river sloping inwards to support them. The stones are not local sandstone of the moor, and must have been brought from some distance, a difficult feat in antiquity.

Throughout history they have been kept in repair because of their value as a crossing place. Countless times they must have been washed away and then laboriously repaired. They were swept away in 1942 by floodwaters, and we saw the damage wrought. But they were soon repaired. Now their value is mainly antiquarian - whether they are prehistoric or mediaeval - set in a wild and lonely spot.

After lunch by the river and paddling about watching the trout and an occasional salmon leap, we returned the way we had come through the woods to Dulverton where we had tea. We were flagging by then and the last two miles to the station seemed endless. We recovered a bit in the train for the walk home. In all eighteen miles. We were very pleased with ourselves. Nipper didn't recover for several days and was immune to the call of 'walks'.

Later that first summer we hired a coach for the day at the end of August and spent the day on the moors. That summer almost all the children and the staff were with us, and a large party set out with picnic lunch in haversacks and baskets. We went first to Tarr Steps for the non-walkers and small children to see. And then up the steep slope of Winsford Hill, pausing at the top to see the large five foot high Celtic Caractacus stone at the cross roads, before turning left for Exford, where we ate our lunch overlooking the village. Exford is right in the centre of the moor, the centre, in peacetime of the Exmoor staghounds. After lunch we continued over the moor to the Doone valley, where we had tea at the so-called Lorna Doonne farm on the banks of the Badgworthy riiver beside an ivy-covered bridge. Tea was set out at a long trestle table in the sun. I have a photograph of it taken with my box brownie, and surprisingly to see today, the ladies were all wearing hats. After tea we visited the isolated Oare church on the edge of the moor where John Ridd was married to Lorna Doone. From Oare we continued down to the main Barnstable Minehead road and went home the quick road through Porlock, Dunster, then due south along the infant Exe to Bampton and home. What a long and exciting day. It was our holiday that year, for in 1940 the first summer of the war, we didn't, like most families in Britain, go away.

Later in the war we walked again to Tarr Steps, and were waiting on the platform at Dulverton station for the train home, tired and weary after eighteen miles on foot. The last train was due at any minute and we were sitting waiting. In the far distance was the sound of a train travelling fast, and the steam could be seen rushing towards us. It approached rapidly, obviously our train from the time point of view, equally obviously not going to stop. We watched in open-mouthed admiration as father jumped bravely down on to the line and waved his stick furiously in the face of the on-coming monster bearing down upon him rapidly. He was shouting something loudly at the top of his voice, which we perhaps fortunately couldn't hear above the din and looking very cross and full of righteous indignation. The train stopped and there was an exchange of words between the driver and father; the station master who had informed us of this train having prudently arranged an engagement elsewhere. 'Public right of transport', 'not in the timetable', 'own railway shares', 'doesn't entitle you to stop any train you please', floated over to us. However, it ended well. Not only were we allowed to travel by the train, we were also welcomed inside the engine to see the works.

Apart from walks locally and further afield, as we grew older we went off on our bicycles carrying picnics with us. Our longest ride was to Wellington Beacon, on its hill above the town, a high monument erected to Lord Wellington in a prominent place some 850 feet up, and visible for miles around. It was open and we were able to climb to the top up rather rickety steps. In those days one was much more likely to be able to go up a monument than one is nowadays when they have to be locked for fear of vandals. We went along the main road to Milverton and south to Wellington, and then decided to go back across country, very rashly, although we had a tattered map. All signposts had been removed for fear of invasion, and even with signposts the tiny back lanes of Devon are most confusing. Instead of being a short cut we must have covered twice the mileage home, unexpectedly travelling through Holcombe Rogus and Ashbrittle, which didn't seem possible, but evidently was. How tired and weary we were that night.

Two or three times a term we went to Taunton on a Saturday to take Harry out after lunch. If it was a wet day we sometimes went in the couny museum, housed in the grounds of the old castle. The most interesting feature to us was the reconstruction of an ancient village near Glastonbury, and the illustration of the way of life of the inhabitants. As far as we were concerned it was best to draw a decent veil over the later history of Taunton, a town which stood for Parliament in the Civil War, and which had backed the Duke of Monmouth's abortive rebellion in 1685 before his defeat at the Battle of Sedgemoor. I went only once to Sedgemoor when I stayed with a school friend who lived on a farm near West Zoyland. It was in winter, and the moor seemed a wild and dreary place, flat and marshy with low hillocks rising above it.

Our parents found the constant presence of the school a strain, month after month, and by August 1941 were ready for a break. Unlike schools under normal conditions, many of the children did not go home for the holidays, so there was always someone with us. We were very fortunate in being able to go away each year, except for 1940.

In August 1941 we went to Minehead for a fortnight's holiday by the sea, and liked it so much that we went also in 1942 and 1943. In the early 1940's it was a small seaside resort, owned largely by the Luttrell family of Dunster Castle, in a wonderful situation on the Bristol Channel. The moors come right down to the town, and the old part by the quay is backed by hills falling steeply into the sea. Looking southward in the distance can be seen Dunkery Beacon, at 1704 feet, the highest point on Exmoor. In August the moors have a purple look about them both close to and from a distance, being covered with flowering heather. Below Dunkery hill is the well-wooded valley around Luccombe, and below again the lower wooded slopes of the mooor. West of Minehead is a wide valley to Porlock which carries the main road along the south coast of the Bristol Channel. This road cuts of North Hill, an offshoot of the moor. Every first evening of our holiday we climbed North Hill. We stayed in a small hotel behind the front and walked north to the delightful fishing village which huddles round the harbour on the slopes of the hill. Like Mevagissey the fishing village suffered in the mid-19th. century when the herrings left and the port was left to silt up. Now there are a few fishing boats, chiefly for visitors. There is an attractive row of small fishermens' cottages, red and yellow and white and various colours leading up to small shops, cafes and a tall towered church where we used to go on Sunday mornings. The father of a school friend of Harry's was the vicar then.

Behind the quay a path leads up to North Hill, winding slowly up in a series of sharp bends through the trees. At the top it continues along the top of the cliffs for about five miles to where the cliffs drop sharply to the west and north at Hurlestone Point, overlooking Porlock Bay. Most of the top of the hill was closed during the war to visitors.

The first summer in Minehead we were still happy on the beach, the wide golden sands stretching roung the bay to Blue Anchor. Harry would have been happy for another year or two of digging on the beach, but after 1941 we had a compromise, beach in the morning, and the rest of the day walking or exploring somewhere else. So over the years we got to know the immediate neighbourhood well. Dunster was always a favourite, with its castle above the small town, still inhabited by the same family after 800 years. We went in the castle grounds, but it was years later that I remember being able to go in the house itself. Perhaps it was not open to the public then. Apart from the unique Yarn Market in the wide main street, there was a lovely walled garden beside the church, which had formerly been part of an abbey's lands, the prior's garden before the dissolution of the monasteries. In the garden was a huge round dovecote and a mediaeval tithe barn. In the street leading to the church was one of the abbey buildings still in use, a gaunt grey slate-tiled house.

Once each summer we took the bus to Porlock. Its fishing village, Porlock Weir is tiny, a few cottages on a little land-locked harbour, and one row of small houses on the harbour bar. From here we walked through the wooded hills along a path clinging to the coast, to Culbone Church, reputed to be the smallest church in Britain, at least the smallest parish church, deep in the woods, apparently serving no noticeable village, just a farm and a few cottages. Coleridge, the poet, had once stayed at the old Ship Inn at Porlock Weir. He was writing his poem Kubla Khan, whilst under the influence of opium, when the landlady knocked and announced 'a person from Porlock'. That person from Porlock was responsible for the poem being unfinished.

Another day we would go to Lynton and Lynmouth along the coastal road with the steep moor rising to the south and the red sandstone cliffs dropping down below, a series of steep bends with alternating views of moor and sea. Here the moor comes right down to the sea, and looking at the coast from the sea it appears to rise straight up a thousand feet or more above the cliffs. These two villages are vulnerable both from land and sea, two rivers meeting here from the moors, plunging down rock filled narrow valleys to the sea amidst spectacular scenery, the villages clinging precariously to the steep hillsides.

On Easter Monday 1941 we went to Barnstable for a week, travelling by train from Venn Cross. Barnstable was a sleepy little town at the head of the estuary of the Taw which had silted up about 100 years before, and it had an attractive bridge across the wide river. It is a centre for the countryside round about and had in those days a market on Fridays in a large covered Victorian market hall, to which we went. We explored the country in the immediate neighbourhood on foot. One day we set out after breakfast with a packed lunch and climbed Godden Hill which rises abruptly from sea level to over 600 feet. It is the western end of a low range of hills on the east bank of the Taw south of Barnstable, and from the top there are magnificent views over Exmoor to the north and the coast from Baggy Point to Hartland. In the distance Lundy could be seen. The river Taw wound below with its wide estuary and the miles of Braunton Burrow sands beyond, haunts of Stalky and Co. and Kipling's unhappy schooldays. We took Stalky and Co. with us to read. We went one day to Appledore at the confluence of the Taw and Torridge, with its narrow streets and painted cottages, and walked from there along a narrow road and over the pebbles to Westward Ho itself. A very bleak spot on a windy day, with miles of shingle in every direction. Another day we went along the Torridge to Bideford, a sleepy little former shipbuilding town. Men from here fought against the Spanish Armada and cannons from the Armada are in the park by the quay. It was here that Charles Kingsley wrote Westward Ho! which we read on our return home.

The thing we enjoyed most about this short holiday and which we talked about afterwards, was the fact that for the first time in our lives we stayed up to dinner at night, feeling very grown up.

During the war we were not able to see much of our northern relations. Some older cousins came once or twice during the summer holidays, but mother was anxious to see her sisters and her younger sister's two little girls whom we had not yet seen. So in 1943 at the end of the summer term, mother and I went up to Bolton to stay with them and visit all our relations. We enjoyed our visit - a great contrast to Devon - but they too had moors above the town.

Mother and father.

Minehead – father, mother, Harry, Nancy and Hugh.

Nancy & father.

Harry.

Chapter 11.   THE WAR

For all we have and are

>For all we have and are
>For all our children's fate,
>Stand up and take the war.
>The Hun is at the gate!
>
>There is but one task for all -
>One life for each to give.
>What stands if Freedom fall?
>Who dies if England live?
>   Rudyard Kipling

On Sept. 3rd. 1939 we had been on holiday in Heysham on the southern shore of Morecombe Bay when war broke out. It was a Sunday morning and we were in church at 11 o'clock, having just arrived for Matins. On arrival the priest went up to the pulpit and announced that we were now at war with Germany. Instead of Matins we were asked to turn to a rarely used portion of the Book of Common Prayer, A Commination or denouncing of God's anger and judgments against sinners. This is a very impressive denunciation of sinners and a call to repentance, appointed to be used on the first day of Lent. The 3rd. September 1939 is the only occasion so far in my life when I have been present at this service. The first part of the service consists of God's cursing against impenitent sinners, taken from Deuteronomy, and the congregation follows each curse by an Amen, 'to the intent that, being admonished of the great indignation of God against sinners, ye may the rather be moved to earnest and true repentance; and may walk more warily in these dangerous days'. Surprisingly few of the curses are no longer relevant in the 20th. century, and the service doubtless provoked salutary thoughts amongst the adults in the congregation. For Harry and I it was a welcome change from Matins and we joined in eagerly. Possibly most of the congregation was cursing Germany in their hearts although this is a commination primarily for the individaul sinner who is exhorted to reform his ways. The perils of sin are clearly enumerated 'He (God) shall pour down rain upon the sinners, snares, fire and brimstone, storm and tempest; this shall be their portion'. Following the curses and thier reward we knelt down and said one of the penitential psalms, number 51, and finished with prayers appealing to God's mercy. Food for thought. We left church with chastened mein.

It was the war which caused us to move to Devon, and the war formed the background to our life there, ever present in our minds and our condition of life. Physically we were not, of course, affected by the war like people living in the big cities. We were in deep country and were at the receiving end of the evacuees. Apart from the school who came to us, in 1940 most farms and cottages received children from London into their homes. For the most part the children came from poor homes and had never been out of London, except possibly for a day trip. Adjustment to country living took time, and understanding on the part of the families who took in the children. Far the greater number benefitted from their few years in the country, and returned home fit and strong. One family arrived, a mother and her six children, one a baby. They were housed in the old school, a tiny building in the centre of the village. She arrived with the main group, bundled out of London for safety, and her husband was a 'dee-briss worker' on the bomb sites, a quiet man who used to come down periodically. His wife had spent her entire life in east London, and was quite unable to cope with country living. She was used to popping out to the shop on the corner several times a day. But here there was no shop, and it needs some organisation to be able to manage with deliveries once a week. She kept running out of essential supplies and could never manage to order enough. Unfortunately her relations and friends were no longer around, and although neighbours were friendly there was mutual suspicion. She used to trail down the road to us or send the eldest boy, George, for a quarter of tea or a packet of cornflakes. We tried to help her by employing George as an assistant gardener to father. I doubt if he had previously set foot in a private garden, and he had no idea how to use simple tools. After pinning his own foot to the ground through the edge of his shoe with the large fork, he was put to cleaning shoes. This he did for some weeks until it was felt his use of polish was too liberal. He was always cheerful, and life at home as the eldest cannot have been easy. Once when father called, the baby was screaming, having fallen off the sofa two days before. He arranged for the doctor to come, who diagnosed a dislocated hip. The baby recovered and flourished, but had a suspicious look on his face as if he never knew what to expect next. As his mother said 'We're all alright except the baby. He doesn't know what the hell to do with himself in the country.' He was six months old at the time. We could always find out what the mother wanted or needed by asking what the baby thought. He was their mouthpiece. Early in 1943 they left, back to the safety of their life in London, only the older children with some regret for what they could see was a better life.

The evacuees were meant to bring with them a case with a change of underclothing, towel, soap, toothbrush and a coat. The ones who came to Clayhanger came with nothing. They had no under-clothes let alone a second set, and few, if any, had a coat. Some had a jacket of their father's cut down to fit them. The country people who received them were shocked at their plight, and also at their thinness, many suffering from rickets. The war did one good thing, and that was to give identical rations to all, so that many people ate properly for the first time, and some of these town children had fresh milk and eggs in abundance for the first time in their lives. They soon grew sturdy and strong and rosy-cheeked.

Our food situation in the countryside was better than most. Throughout the war and long afterwards we kept hens, free range, in a corner of the tithe barn field. Unfortunately they were only allowed two sacks of corn a year. Mostly they grumbled over boiled up potato and vegetable peelings, and scratched frantically for any tasty morsel. As a result the egg yield was low. But the eggs themselves were delicious with their thick brown shells. When they got too old to lay they were boiled up themselves and produced chicken broth and pies. We grew all our own vegetables and fruit. Otherwise our rations were the same as in towns, except for the year of the foot and mouth epidemic, when we had an unexpected supply of meat, huge joints of local lamb and beef which we talked of nostalgically for years to come.

Shortly after we arrived a Ministry of Food inspector arrived. He came to tell us that we would be responsible for the emergency store of food for the village in case of invasion. Shortly after, iron rations were delivered, endless huge square tins. These were filled with basic necessities, sugar and flour, butter and dried eggs, meat loaf and large square hard biscuits. All the tins were sealed with an M.O.F. binding, and we were not, of course, allowed to touch them. They remained in a corner of the large attic until collected in December 1943 and sent off to an unknown destination. When our rations were particularly low we used to brood over the tins marked 'butter'. I wonder if the stores supplied to every village were ever used, or if they are still languishing in some warehouse for a future emergency.

In case of invasion the church bells were to be rung as a warning. Invasion was a very real threat especially in the months following Dunkirk, when the Germans were actually in sight across the channel. Serious preparations were made to prepare for this. In every county signposts and all milestones were removed. Some milestones had been there since the Romans, and 1940 saw the disappearance of the larger number of these stones. They were taken away never to return. Some counties have been conscientious in replacing milestones, and Dorset has more than any other county in situ. Also their signposts are model ones. Each signpost has the name of the crossroads or corner, or nearest village at the top, plus the National Grid reference, so that it can easily be found on the ordance survey map.

North Devon is criss-crossed by a network of tiny roads, meandering through the countryside from village to village, and converging on market towns. In 1940 all signposts were removed, and this meant that as soon as one was away from ones immediate neighbourhood, say four or five miles, one could very easily get lost. The fact that a road appeared to go in the right direction was no guarantee that it actually arrived at the desired destination. We were quite familiar with the layout of the land within walking distance, and there are many notable landmarks in Devon, but walking along a deeply sunk lane it is difficult to find a landmark to recognize. One struggled up the bank only to see a few tiny fields surrounded by equally high banks and hedges and inhabited by indifferent cows.

We were all impressed by the invasion propaganda issued for our protection. 'Walls have ears' was one of the slogans. We gave information to strangers furtively in a whisper if at all. In the train travelling with country women and their huge baskets we preserved a dignified silence on the subject of where we were, unless we knew everyone in the carriage. All stations were blacked out and the names laboriously removed. Our station was easy to recognize coming from Taunton, as there were two tunnels and a long viaduct between it and Wiveliscombe. But sometimes there was confusion at the others. 'Is this Milverton?' a dear old lady with a local accent and bulging shopping basket asked a passing porter, only to be greeted by a suspicious look. She turned to us for help, and our faces assumed the 'I am a stranger here' look so often encountered when seeking information in an unknown town.

Occasionally we made expeditions by car. Mrs. Peerless, Mary's mother who lived at a neighbouring farm during the war, kept her car in our garage, and was generous with lifts when petrol was available. We also had Mr. Hannam. Late in 1940 our parents and Miss Widlake had to visit Wellington for the dentist, and there was no other way of getting there. We had been told ad nauseum to trust no one, Germans would arrive in heavy disguise. Here was a car full of perfect suspects. What more obvious disguise than that of a clerical collar? Seated beside this obvious fake was Miss Widlake, crippled as a child, another disguise. Even more suspicious in front were Hannam, driving, and mother with a swollen face. Hannam had a closely cropped hairstyle, evidently showing his true colours, and not bothering about disguises. After four or five miles across country, they no longer knew the way, and although there was a large-scale map in the car, it was not of much use in the heart of Devon unless accompanied by one or two signposts. They stopped and asked a hedger. He sized them up pretty smartly, and got on with his work looking suspiciously at them over his shoulder when they produced the map. We all knew about the Germans who had been here as 'harmless' tourists in the 1930's, taking photos of our bridges and roads to make maps on their return. Although we never completely understood why they did not buy our excellent large-scale maps freely available at all stationers. They went on and stopped in an unnamed village with no more success. A journey of some ten miles took them an hour and a half. After treatment at the dentist they attempted to return in the dark, with equal success. It was nearly 10 p.m. by the time they got home to find us all waiting up anxiously.

Preparations were made in case of invasion. Quite apart from fighting in the hedges and ditches and on the beaches, and only yielding our country inch by inch as exhorted by Churchill, practical preparations were also made, concerning food and other supplies. The school to which I went in Taunton was to be used as a hospital in case of invasion, and we were anxious that they should fill it with beds and prepare in plenty of time so that we needn't go any more. The sirens went once or twice while we were at school, and we all foregathered with our gasmasks in the cloakrooms. Periodically we sat with the masks on and continued our lessons during an imaginary gas attack. Always we carried them with us bumping on our backs with our satchels. In our pockets we carried Identity cards, which became an inseparable part of us. Occasionally it would be accidently washed with the garment containing it, to emerge ever more limp and dog-eared. No one ever demanded to see mine, or asked for my identity number. Inside it I carried my sweet coupons, a much more valuable item, changed each week into one or two ounces of crunchie bar at a shop on the way to school, occasionally laboriously saved for a luxurious birthday present.

The local Home Guard were to be our protection in case of invasion, and we put our trust in them, quite happily, a band of tough countrymen, exposed since childhood to all the elements in their hard lives on the land. Perhaps a shade old, some too young, but reliable and trustworthy. Father joined the local guard as soon as it was formed. They had to have partners, and he chose his sexton Fred Curtis. As he said, Fred Curtis had worked on the land since he was thirteen, and could turn his hand to anything, and if he had to spend a night outside in a field he would rather be with someone who could cope. The first night they spent out was in the field across the road. So instead of cold rations and making do, we went over with a flask of hot soup and later a pot of tea. Early in the morning they staggered in bleary eyed to make more tea. It was taking too long for their kettle to boil on the damp twigs they'd lit at dawn when the curfew on lights came off.

The Home Guard were very conscious of the dangers oof invasion. They had practises with neighbouring villages, and went on what were grandly termed manoeuvres. The farmers had a different name for them when people were expected to have paid time off to indulge in 'them carryings on'. One day we were expecting an invasion by the Huntsham Home Guard. At least the relations of the Home Guard were. It was meant to be a closely guarded secret. Our Home Guard stationed themselves in the fields and hedges round Bonny Cross in plenty of time to intercept the enemy on their arrival. But they were foiled. We in the village watched the Huntsham men arrive quite openly from a different direction, and go on up to Bonny Cross to rout our men in the rear. A total disaster.

Father was out with the Home Guard the night Plymouth was raided and the night Exeter was severely bombed. In both cases he saw the glare of burning buildings, and in the case of Exeter, he heard the distant fall of bombs. One night at 2 a.m. we were woken by a bomb. The house shook and one or two windows cracked. We all gathered on the landing, the smaller children in tears. It was obviously a pilot getting rid of his load, so we all went back to bed. Exactly an hour later a time bomb went off with a much greater impact. We all rushed down into the kitchen and spent the rest of the night huddled beneath the large wooden table. It didn't occur to anyone to go down into the damp and noisesome cellar which had been prepared for just such an eventuality by digging an entrance into the garden. In the heart of the country one didn't expect to have any warning as we were out of reach of sirens.

Sometimes people ask 'what would you save, if you could only take one thing?', and one thinks of one's most valuable possession. Most of the children arrived in the kitchen clutching their bears. Father toured the house to see if everyone was down, ând arrived carrying in his hand the Elizabeth chalice and paten in its original leather case. He said the records would have to take their chance as he couldn't manage the tin trunk which housed them. The chalice was probaly the one completely irreplaceable item in the house, kept beneath father's bed as being safer there than in the open church.

The following day we found that the bombs had fallen in a field south of Featherbed Lane opposite a bungalow where an old widow lived alone. There was not much left of the bungalow, but she had escaped unhurt. One of the craters was sixty feet across and quite changed the appearance of the field, which the farmer was ruefully regarding. All the village was up there collecting bomb fragments and speculating as to whether we could expect any more 'raids'. One or two people said that they had been expecting it. They had seen signalling lights. Every night there had been lights flashed from the top of the hill beyond Bonny Cross, signalling to enemy aircraft passing overhead en route to Exeter or Plymouth. It was rumoured that a group of enemy agents were camping out in the woods. Others claimed to have seen lights from the hill behind our house, looking suspiciously at us, the latest newcomers. We hotly denied all knowledge of any such activities. For weeks after we looked in vain for any lights. We also practised the morse code with our torches in case we were ever cut off by the enemy and had to signal for help. These were the first and last bombs to fall anywhere near, and our closest brush with the war.

Periodically the Home Guard would have a church parade. In that case father left off his private's uniform, and acted in his other capacity as chaplain to the Clayhanger Home Guard. They would foregather in the village, and march smartly into church and up to the front pews reserved for them. One dreadful occasion the organist didn't turn up. As she lived some miles away there was no question of fetching her. She kept the organ locked and the key at home unless arrangements had been made for another organist to play in her place. Miss Widlake was a good pianist and always ready to step into the breach, and one of the children would 'blow' in an emergency to provide the power. The congregation were seated and the approach of the Home Guard could be heard. Father sent home for a hammer and chisel, and frightful sounds of straining wood and forced locks was heard issuing forth from the organ recess. Then the strain of a martial voluntary wafted down the aisle to greet the arrival of our local stalwarts. There was a great roar of the National Anthem, and then a settling down to Evensong with twenty extra men's voices thrown in for good measure.

Later during the war parades were always held on a Sunday and father resigned his private's position while remaining their chaplain. When his uniform was handed in he was very reluctant to part with the boots, 'the best pair of gardening boots I'd have had', he mourned. I wonder what happened to all the second hand boots handed in by the country Home Guard. Many of them must have had their eye on them for future use in field and garden.

During the First World War father had been a very young subaltern with the Border Regiment fighting in France. At one time he was made Despatch Officer, a very unlikely role for him to fill. He is the least mechanically minded of men, and has never driven a car nor ridden a bicycle. He was the fourth son, and all the others had bicycles. But father used to stroll along as a child either deep in a book or deep in thought, and it was felt far too dangerous a risk to the lives of others to allow him to mount a bike. Many years later we tried in vain to teach him. In France he rejected the offer of motor transport, attempted to ride a bike, and finished up with a horse. He could at least ride a horse, but apart from the cavalry regiments, there was only a poor selection of horses available for anyone else. The horse he was given had only one thought in mind, his nosebag. The first time father went off with his despatches, he left the horse outside to deliver them, and when he came out it was gone, back to its manger. Next time he remembered to tie it up. The horse had two speeds, slow going out, fast coming back. Once they had trundled some two miles when the horse decided definitely not to go any further. He turned round and began his second speed of racing the clock back to the stables. At the time the Border Regiment were billetted in an old chateau in a park, and the entrance to the stable block led through an old stone arch. Some half mile away father realized two things, that he would be decapitated if he rode into the yard, and the other, that he was quite unable to stop the one-track idea beneath him. As they galloped up the drive he flung himself full length along the horse and clung for dear life beneath its chin. A very undignified entrance for the despatch officer. It was the last time he went. He willingly offered to deliver anything on foot, but if speed was required they would have to choose someone else. We still have a photo of him in those days, a smart young man with his puttees and boots and moustache, father twenty years before we first remember him clearly.

We were all very patriotic during the war, and patriotism was still taught as a virtue in our schools. When I first went to Taunton to school, I joined the junior League of Nations which met after school. We were still at the centre of the mightiest empire in the history of the world, and everyone knew people who served abroad, spending their lives in service to India or Burma, Egypt or the Far East, some tiny island, or who had emigrated to one of the Dominions, Canada, Australia or South

Africa. Pride in the Empire was encouraged, and we cheered the Gurkha troops, and the contingents from Africa and the Dominions who came to share our plight.

There were War Weapons Weeks periodically, when processions were held in Taunton. One I remember was on 15th. February 1941 when we went to take Harry out for the afternoon, and we spent the whole time in the main street watching the weapons pass, guns, tanks and marching men. How proud we were of them. There were also National days of Prayer, Sundays set aside to pray especially for peace, when more would come to church to pray for those they knew and loved who had gone to fight. We thought of Tullie and Sam, whom we had known in Cambridge, punting on the Cam. Later Tullie was killed in a tank in North Africa, a chaplain, but right in the front line. Sam was taken prisoner at Dunkirk. Then there was Geoffrey Mowat, son of father's old tutor at Oxford, who had gone out in the Colonial Service to Malaya as a young man just before the war. His wife came back on the last ship from Singapore, and he disappeared into the notorious Changi Jail, and later laboured on the nightmare railway through the jungle. His mother had painted our house in 1940. Years later I married a man who had been in the same form with him at school. The father of the three Bayly's who lived with us, walked 500 miles out of Burma to the safety of India.

Harry fancied himself as a poet, and wrote a patriotic poem in 1942 at the age of eleven: <u>Fight On</u>

>Fight on, fight on
>For our country and King
>Fight on, fight on
>'Tis a glorious thing
>If you want to help your country and King
>Save all scrap metal, paper and string.
>Fight on, fight on
>Against the Hun until
>This glorious victory's won.

We used to be keen on war games, and were usually fighting some imaginary battle, but usually from the age of chivalry. One Christmas we received a board game called Dover Patrol, which we played for years, the board a seascape and the pieces ships and mines of opposing fleets.

The war saw the end of the ancient Anglican parochial system of virtually one priest for every church throughout the country, however small the parish. A very good system for pastoral care, with the priest nnormally staying many years and really knowing his parishoners. But change was in the wind. The old system of parsonage and church and resident priest in every place was gone never to return, and it has yet to be seen whether the system or group of systems which replaced it will further the cause of Christianity as well as the old. The great drawback to the clergy themselves is the loss of time, time for reading and study. Until 1914 the minimum requirements for Oxford and Cambridge where the bulk of future clergy took their degrees, was Latin and Greek and Greek New Testament. Father read the New Testament in Greek as naturally as in English, and spent several hours a day in study. Of course this stopped during the war years, and since the war clergy have in many cases been far too busy to be able to devote more than an hour or two a day to their study of the scriptures and theology. A loss for themselves, and a far greated loss to the people they serve.

Chapter 12.   POSTCRIPT

                        The Countryman in Exile

                I travelled among unknown men,
                In lands beyond the sea;
                Nor, England! did I know till then
                What love I bore to thee.

                'Tis past, that melancholy dream!
                Nor will I quit thy shore
                A second time; for still I seem
                To love thee more and more.
                                William Wordsworth.

After more than a quarter of a century I revisited Clayhanger on 16th. September 1972, as an unexpected opportunity occurred. It has stood the test of time. In my memory over the years the time we spent there was crystallizeed into an image of perfection. For years after leaving I couldn't bear to think of it because of not being able to live there. And then I went to the university and soon after to the Middle East. During the years in the Middle East, Clayhanger was the symbol of England. In the hot and dusty countries of Egypt and Iraq, the cool Devon countryside with its sparkling rivers was an unattainable mirage. Then we returned home, but to eastern England. In 1972 we returned to the west, to Dorset. We went to Exbridge near Dulverton to collect plants and shrubs from the nurseries along the Exe below the bridge. From Taunton we took the well-known road to Venn Cross closely linked to the railway. The line is up but the little stations remain, some with the station master still living in his small house beside the line as in the case of Venn Cross. (In 1972). Through Norton Fitzwarren, with its cider apple orchards, and on through Milverton, an elegant Georgian village with houses fronting onto the original cobbled street with the road below, the first sight of a red sandstne church with tall tower, and a road cutting through deep sandstone banks. Then along the railway across which lay the Brendon Hills, well-wooded. Facing the railway along the hill, three farmhouses as I remembered them, the middle one wooden. All surrounded by apple orchards. Then to Wiveliscombe, smaller than I remembered, with its high church tower, and one or two old houses and shops beside the road. Beyond, the road leaves the railway and climbs steeply several hundred round knife-edged hairpin bends. Then the slow descent through wooded lanes to Waterrow beside the Tone, with its cafe where we used to go as a treat to eat boiled eggs for tea. Beyond could be seen the high viaduct of the railway, now largely dismantled except for the piers. Here in the bungalow on the right lived Hannam. I wonder if he is still there. A mile or two further and we left the road to Clayhanger on the left, and Venn Cross on the right. Four miles on to Shillingford with apparently no new buildings. Just before the village the gaunt Victorian redbrick school, still in use. Then Shillingford itself, a short street with delightful pub 'The Barleycorn' with an inn sign of a mouse in the barley. Then off the road to Exbridge along a real Devon lane of high banks and no signposts. Near Morebath we crossed the one track railway, the beginning of the branch line to Exeter from Morebath Junction Halt - where the train stopped to let the sheep go by so long ago. It seemed unreal.

At Exbridge the wide and sparkling Exe with its trout and salmon and 17th. century three-span bridge. The old Anchor Inn overlooks the stream and Panton's nurseries beyond. We ate our picnic beside the river and watched a fisherman. Deep silence apart from the river. Still quite unspoilt. I have lived happily beside the Tigris, and near the Nile and Jordan, mighty and loved rivers, but in my mind the Exe and Barle have always been the best, wide and shallow with pools and rushes, rapids and bridges, and the deep wooded combes of the upper reaches where the red deer live. We bought our shrubs and set off for home.

We left the road at Petton and round the first corner was the Victorian church with its single bell tower. Harvest Festival tomorrow and cars outside. We went in and there were fifteen women decorating. The church was newly white-washed and everywhere shining clean and loved. Piles of fruit and vegetables, corn and barley. We spoke to a woman. She was Winnie's sister and father had christened her baby. 'Not Mr. O'Neill Drew's daughter' she exclaimed. She brought over Mrs. Palfrey, Joyce's mother. How pleased we were to see each other again! Mrs. Palfrey told me that her daughter was dead, aged forty-five, a year ago. So she was only a few years older than me when she came to work for us, and I was twelve, and I remember her as one of the 'big girls'. 'You must call on Winnie', they said.

We went along the well-known road. Nothing new. A sudden distant view of Clayhanger church with its high tower silhouetted against the sky. What a long winding road through deep banks. The watersplash has gone, replaced by a culvert. Outside the farms the same wooden stands with the milk churns. The fields all pasture, steep, some thistly. Full of cows. The steeper fields with sheep. All with trees and copses, Nutcombe Copse the largest. Then Bonny Cross and Featherbed Lane, just the same. The roads the same within their deep banks, the only change being that the hedges had been cut by mechanical hedge cutter and not by hand of the hedger and ditcher of my childhood. Not an improvement! Left at the crossroads, past the small telephone exchange and down into the village. There it was unchanged, as though the clock had turned back thirty years. Not a single new building. On the left the two semi-detached council houses where Winnie had lived with her mother, then the old school, and opposite a shop. That was new. Opposite again two lovely cottages with real cottage gardens, a riot of colour, rich and bright. I stopped here to call on Winnie while John took the boys to the church. I knocked and she came hurrying round from the garden. Why, she was just the same! It couldn't be possible. Then I realized that she looked like her mother had looked when we were there. In my memory she was a young woman and I was a school girl. We didn't of course know each other, but we had known each other well so long ago. We smiled and talked. 'Do you remember?' we asked each other. 'Do you remember poor old Pringle?', the old man from the post office. Now Winnie's son has the shop and that is a great improvement in the village, to have a shop. Her mother had lived to be ninety.

John and the boys returned from the church where the boys had liked the mounting block. Also they had been pleased to see their grandfather's name on the list of rectors. We went on down the hill, past the turning to Nutcombe, to the stream at the bottom of our drive. Here was a change - it was almost dry! Devon had had an unprecedented drought in 1972, and everywhere was less green, the streams smaller and no rich red mud round the field entrances. The rectory had changed outwardly very much. It had recently been sold. The bottom drive was overgrown and the lawns gone. One could no longer see the house from the road. The well was open and filled with rubble. The tithe barn beyond looked the same. One day I hope to return and call to see the house.

On up the hill along which I walked to school through the deep banks. We ate our picnic on the bank beside Well Hayes apple orchards. No traffic, no sound, deep and peaceful quiet. But there is a change. There is a pylon in a gap between the hills, one of a line. But not an unwelcome change this, electricity, which came in 1951. Then up through the winding lanes to the top of Well Hayes hill and the view of the valley and the Brendon Hills beyond. Not spectacular tourist scenery. Rolling hills and small valleys, copses and streams, tiny fields and red soil. Cows and sheep in their fields, pigs and hens near the farmyards. Small farms and small cottages, cheerful gardens. England as one remembers it abroad.

When we came back from the Middle east, we found great changes in Britain, particularly in the countryside. The steam trains had gone, local lines closed, roads carried heavy traffic, motorways scored the country. Building went on apace, ugly buildings pushing out into the countryside. And, very strange, returning from biblical scenes of shepherds with their sheep, the disappearance of many animals from their fields into batteries, particularly hens, but also, disturbingly pigs and calves and even sheep, doomed to spend their lives in cramped and unnatural conditions because of man's greed.

What a relief to see that change hadn't touched one small piece of England, only a few miles from busy tourist routes, but essentially the same as a quarter of a century ago. In some respects with the going of the railway, reverting to an even earlier Britain.

I do not hanker to live there now. The scene is the same, but life has changed, and the players, of whom I was one, are gone. I'm happy it is still unchanged and beautiful, with the same country people remaining as their ancestors before them, living the same lives in an era of violence and disturbance, the yeomen of England.

I wrote this postcript in 1972, and put the manuscript away. Now in October 1989 my brother Harry has died suddenly at the age of 58. I came across it in the loft and thought I would copy it out for his children - the wartime childhood we spent so happily in Clayhanger long ago. And I dedicate it to his memory - my fellow conspirator.

Return August 1990

Sometime in February I sent a copy of Clayhanger to Desmond and Ann Collins, and in August Ann invited us to stay a night. We had a lovely time, far beyond what I imagined, as it is a risk to return to a place where one has been very happy. It is only 55 miles from where we live in Dorset. We picniced in a churchyard near Taunton, and then went along the Barnstable road running alongside the disused railway - so the view was much the same as that which I saw from the train as a child. At Venn Cross we turned into the well-remembered road. Left John here to walk the was I went home from school. There is very little change - the houses less shabby, and the ubiquitous Friesian has replaced the old Red Devon. The walk seemed shorter, even though I was imagining Mother and Father and Harry, and Nipper running on ahead with a stick. The Tithe Barn has become the W.I. Hall where I waited for John. Entered by upper gate and walked round to front door.

Ann very friendly and welcoming and took us up to parents' old room, with bathroom attached! Luxury. Bathroom seemed familiar - i.e. view from window (nothing else!) It is the old bathroom which was so bleak in 1939 with bare boards and tin hip bath, bucket, wooden screen and towel horse. The bedroom was the same in many ways, same windows and big cupboard where mother kept the linen. A room with good proportions. It was very moving to see the lovely well-remembered view of the garden and fields beyond. I had not been upstairs in the house since we left in 1943. Windows the same in lounge, and shutters, still painted white. Lounge has now merged with little sitting room which still has french windows into courtyard. Courtyard very changed, with flags and no cherry tree, or wall into the vegetable garden. The house looks well - different, because paint has gone and stones revealed which is a big improvement. Marks of old door in corner of angle of wall turn out to be door into larder from kitchen - now gone. Appearance of windows of both sides of the house the same from courtyard. Woodshed the same - with white-washed wall of house on one side. Felt nostalgic and remembered all father's tools hanging on the walls and all the wood waiting to be sawn up and the wooden 'horses'

The front of the house is rendered, a brownish colour, which makes it look different. No verandah - which makes the rooms hot in sunny summers, says Ann. The greenhouse has gone, and also the wall on the other side with its door to the vegetable garden; and the thick hedge which ran from the wall to the field. Also the gate to the field, to which there is now no access from the garden. The lower lawn has croquet laid out. Old croquet lawn now under wider drive. Lower drive very much the same, and little path through the trees. Saw Winnie Tucker coming up the drive for tea. It was good to see her. I have no one to tell who can remember, now my first family are all gone, and we were able to say to each other, 'do you remember ...? We sat in the lounge and ate a delicious tea - how mother would have liked a real tea. Parents used to have tea there with Widdie, wheeled in on the old trolley, while we ate 'doorsteps' and jam in the dining room. When Winnie had gone we went round the house. Dining room now very lovely study for Desmond who is an archaeologist, with door through to passage. Old china cupboard now downstairs cloakroom. Butler's pantry changed out of all recognition, except for former kitchen tiles on the floor. Told them how we used to climb out of window to privy in shed, over winterborne stream - a dash in rainy weather. Later had an elsan in what is now potting shed off courtyard - we wondered about the bulging wall we squeezed past to get to it - now revealed as an old bread oven and fireplace. Kitchen now the dining room, with arch to scullery, now kitchen, with this pleasant fireplace. Back stairs to first floor in same place, open stairs, and not behind door now. The flight of stairs behind door to old nursery are just the same. From there we used to get to garden down steps. A new window in the east wall of the kitchen where the pump stood, makes the room much lighter.

Upstairs, parents room and Miss Widlake's much the same, but Harry's room now -bath room, and my old room a dressing room. Recognize the views over the courtyard. Round corner into old dormitory, now two rooms with windows over vegetable garden. Old parish room now bedroom. Open stairs from kitchen end in remembered banisters, and stained glass window. Glass has survived all these years and Desmond was able to replace a small pane of blue. Up original stairs to old attics. Largest now a playroom, and the others empty. I had quite forgotten one of the rooms down a short flight of stairs, with high ceiling. But remembered the view. This room is on a different level as it is above the old nursery.

Very pleased with house which is cared for and loved. Desmond has an early copy of a Terier signed by Archbishop William Laud about the house dating from 1634. How father would have liked to see it.

Very delicious supper over which we lingered and talked, a treat for us. Enjoyed the vegetables from the garden. (And the meringue banana icecream!)

It was good to sleep in parents' old room and think of them. Lovely view - I realized in childhood the high standard of countryside of Devon. It was very quiet at night - there is a quality of stillness, not so noticeable during the war when there were so many people in the house.

but tonight just the sounds an old house makes as it settles, and the sounds of the countryside. The peace of the garden and the fields.

I meant to get up early and go out, but slept late. After breakfast we walked up to village past old pub (or rather New Inn) to the church. The pipe organ has gone. Strangely it seems large! It is larger than all my churches except Melbury Osmond. I thought of Miss Widlake reading the lessons and the girls sitting in rows below the pulpit, with mother and Harry and I opposite the Sun God. Wonderful carved Elizabethan pew ends. Moved to be there again where I was confirmed.

Walked up to Bonny Cross - only two new houses and one new telephone exchange, and looked at the view - which has changed, but subtly. Over fifty years trees have fallen or been cut down, and though the bones of the landscape are the same the details have altered the picture.

At the end of the lower drive, which is very much the same, saw the old weeping ash on its 'island' no longer surrounded by water. And the little path behind the trees. The well is open, with the pipes which were put in when we were there. Realized how much pumping we had to do to raise the water up the bank and to the attics where the tanks were, and the rush to 'pump' when the level dropped and the hot water began to boil. Across the road the stile has gone which led into the upper field - a right of way to Petton past Nutcombe Manor. (Desmond has now restored it). Ruined cottages now under Dutch barn.

There are two lovely intelligent cats - one black with a red collar, one a light grey tabby. When we went out in the morning and saw them I suddenly thought 'they are the wrong cats'! How ridiculous.

Why was Clayhanger so important to me? Only four years, but important years 11 to 15; conditions unusual being wartime and the school with us. Also the feeling of common purpose in the land - a good feeling of all being involved together.

It was here that I began to love the English countryside, and the people of the land, the real people of England. And also my real job - by observation of what it is to be a country parson - visiting with father certainly. But also seeing him read, his knowledge of history and poetry and gardening. His being what he was called to be.

When we left it took me years to come to terms with the bareness of the Berkshire downs. Nothing ever came up to the standard of Clayhanger again from that point of view. It was a lodestone to me in the Middle East.

Shortly after we arrived and I was going with Father visiting in the afternoons before the school came, I began to realize that I myself had a vocation, although I would'nt have been able to articulate it. I realized then that the life of a country parson is the most fulfilling. Mentioning it once to the parents they laughed - but children are used to being laughed at. At the time of my confirmation I felt the mysterious call surface again. But it was not until the summer after we left Clayhanger that I realized that I was not going to be a parson of any kind as a woman, and this cast a shadow over my life for some years. But this happened after we had left, and no great shadow (except the war!) fell over our lives there.

What was the special quality of this countryside and place - down a lane no one would look at twice hurrying along the Barnstable road towards the moors? The quality which made me remember and love the place all my life? It is to be found elsewhere, but it was here for me. That extra quality of reality, which when perceived through the senses enables belief, belief which may be inarticulate and disregarded, but never cast aside.

It was living there that enabled me to learn the world to be sacramental, filled (ambiguously) with the presence of God. Not to be pinned down and explained, but to be 'read'; land a gift, to be loved and cherished. Realized very clearly by the Jews about Israel. Through the land one may come into communion with God - through food, through animals, through the land itself. Those fortunate enough to spend their childhood in the country learn this naturally.

As children we lived close to the land, with its flowers and trees, animals and birds; its streams and wells, its hills and valleys, and the farms. We learned that there is an individuality and value in animals and plants and rocks in their own existence apart from their usefulness - 'very good', said God! A felt acceptance of the providential givenness of the natural world.

Through closeness to the land you touch (unknowingly) the core of man's relationship with God, for the land is proof of a power in life greater than ourselves. We perhaps realized dimly that the land was related to the source of life. And we were still and listened - and listening and stillness renews and makes whole. We did'nt talk about it. We just became aware of the silence and small sounds of the countryside, and became at home with the quietness of nature. We grew like weeds, roots strong, sharing with the rest of creation. And man, membership of a small community (or two small communities, village and school, intertwined) engaged through all its members in all the chief activities of life, manual, intellectual, social and familial - in common purpose.

In the garden of Eden God brought the animals to Adam to name. To name a thing is to manifest the meaning and value God gave to it. And we did that – we named places – the pleasance – a place of pleasure and relaxation, a little bit of garden not gardened for food, but left for fun – an important name to us. And in the first months the secret streams and paths we found and would not reveal (not that any adult would have been able to go along some of them). To name a thing, is, even if only apprehended dimly, to bless God for it and in it. And this is not a religious act, but a way of life. Man was called to stand at the centre of the world and bless it by his presence – bringing it into communion with God – a priestly vocation. Here at this time some 50 years later I thanked God for this gift I had in childhood. And for now having the words to know what Clayhanger did for me.

Returning after so long, as I was walking from Venn Cross the beauty moved me with scarcely bearable force. The lovely landscape, hearing the birds, smelling the honeysuckle in the banks, feeling the grass underfoot – when do these cease merely to involve the senses? Is it when they give such deep pleasure or consolation that they evoke a response which demands thanksgiving to their creator? Once we become aware of the spiritual dimension we never forget it. It becomes part of us.

The very good thing is that now my beloved and well remembered past is integrated in the present, having with Desmond and Ann made the past present, so that for me at least they exist side by side.

Clayhanger Rectory – plan of garden

Field

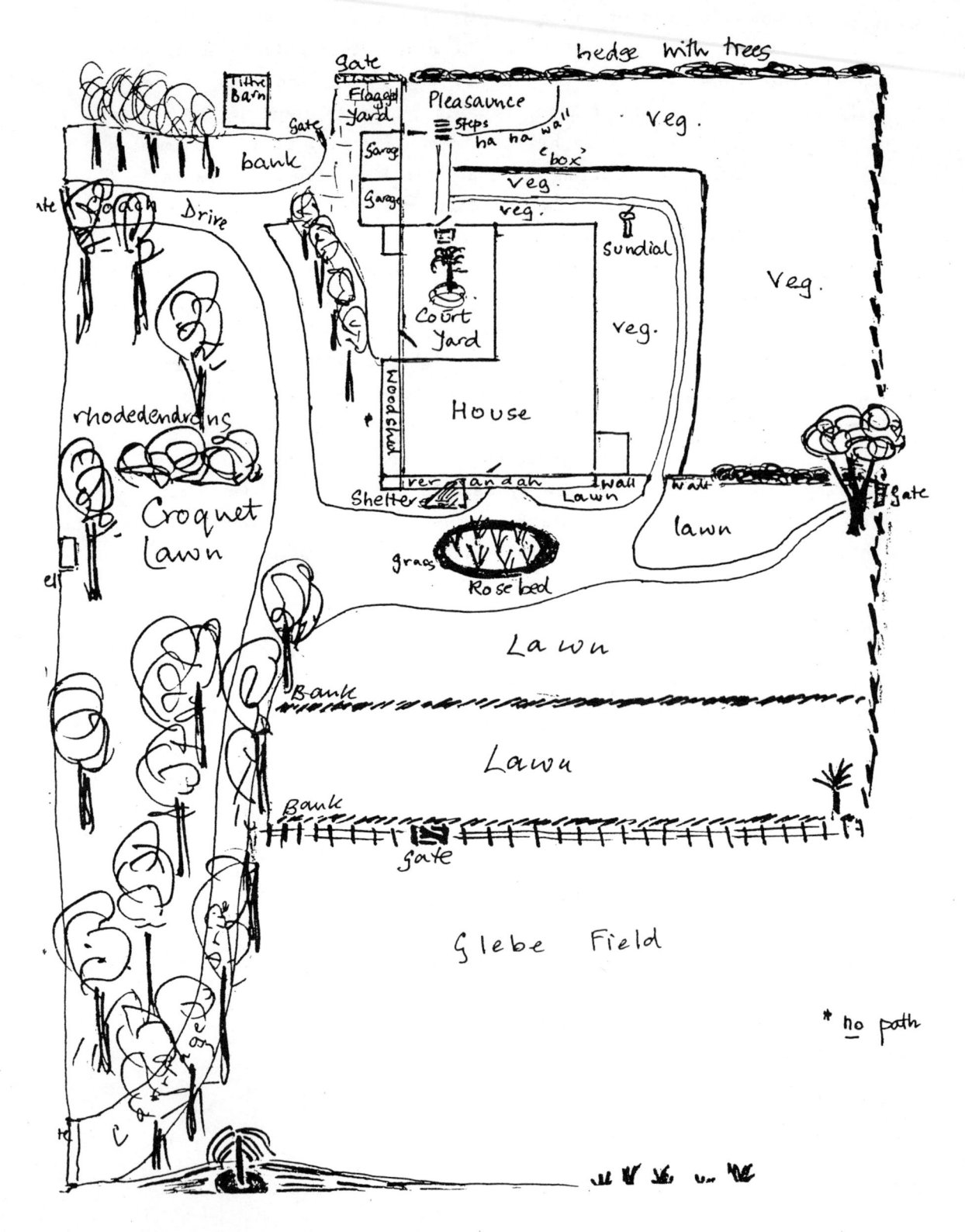

hedge with trees

gate
Tithe Barn
Flagged Yard
Pleasaunce
Steps
ha ha wall
"box"
veg.
bank
Garage
Garage
veg.
gate
Coach
Drive
veg.
sundial
veg.
veg.
Court Yard
rhododendrons
Woodshed
House
Croquet lawn
Shelter
verandah
Wall
Lawn
wall
lawn
gate
grass
Rose bed
Lawn
Bank
Lawn
Bank
gate
Glebe Field

* no path